TIGER

OSPREY
PUBLISHING

GER

Thomas Anderson

OSPREY PUBLISHING
Bloomsbury Publishing Plc

Kemp House, Chawley Park, Oxford OX2 9PH, UK
29 Earlsfort Terrace, Dublin 2, Ireland
1385 Broadway, 5th Floor, New York, NY 10018, USA
Email: info@ospreypublishing.com
www.ospreypublishing.com

OSPREY is a trademark of Osprey Publishing Ltd

First published in Great Britain in 2013

A CIP catalogue record for this book is available from the British Library.

Print ISBN: 978 1 4728 2204 8
ePub: 978 1 78200 292 5
ePDF: 978 1 78200 283 3
XML: 978 1 4728 2977 1

22 23 24 25 26   10 9 8 7 6 5 4 3 2

Conceived and edited by Jasper Spencer Smith.
Design and artwork by Nigel Pell.
Index by William Jack.
Produced by Editworks Limited, Bournemouth BH1 4RT, UK.
Printed and bound in India by Replika Press Private Ltd.

Image acknowledgements

Front cover (top) and title page: A PzKpfw VI Tiger Ausf E in service with 2nd SS-Panzer Division Das Reich advancing towards Kursk during *Unternehmen Zitadelle* (Operation *Citadel*) in summer 1943. (Panzerfoto)

Front cover (bottom): A PzKpfw VI Tiger Ausf B fitted with narrow transport tracks (note the track guards have been removed) to allow ease of movement during transfer by rail. (Getty)

Back cover photo credits (top to bottom): Münch, Münch, Anderson, Topfoto, Panzerfoto.

The Woodland Trust
Osprey Publishing supports the Woodland Trust, the UK's leading woodland conservation charity.

www.ospreypublishing.com
To find out more about our authors and books visit our website. Here you will find extracts, author interviews, details of forthcoming events and the option to sign-up for our newsletter.

CONTENTS

Development 1

There is possibly no other weapon more well known, and more revered than the *Panzerkampfwagen* VI Tiger. In late 1942, when the Tiger was first seen on the battlefield, it was quickly used for propaganda purposes. Of course the national press, now under the control of the Nazi government, used the new tank to pronounce the superiority of German weapons, especially after the defeat of their forces at the Battle of Stalingrad (23 August 1942 to 2 February 1943).

A former German Army officer who had once served with sPzAbt 503 on the Tiger in the East noted:

> We had better tanks. But what was more important, our mission tactics combined with our fighting spirit were clearly superior. When there were no *Jabos* (fighter-bombers), we could easily defeat any *Panzerfeind* (enemy tank) even when outnumbered three to one...

Ironically, the press in Great Britain also did their best to emphasize the effectiveness of German weapons. The 8.8cm FlaK anti-aircraft gun and the Tiger tank were just two which were vaunted in many published articles.

What was it about this tank? Were the many stories true? Did the Tiger really withstand *any* fire? Was the feared 8.8cm gun that effective? And was the Tiger really that unreliable?

It is interesting to follow the development of the Tiger through three different events which were to effect German military planning.

The first can be traced back to the outcome of World War I which ended with the signing of the Treaty of Versailles (one of several treaties made in succession at the end of the war). In brief, Germany was declared responsible for beginning the war. The country had to make great territorial concessions. All former overseas colonies were handed over to the victorious nations

One of eight Tiger Ausf E tanks issued to Tigergruppe Meyer in August 1943. It carries the name "Strolch" (Vagabond) and is painted with a dark yellow base camouflaged with olive green and possibly red brown stripes. A single-digit turret numbering system was chosen for this small combat unit. The shield with a Baltenkreuz (German cross), painted on the front plate, was adapted for this Tigergruppe. (Münch)

The T-34 was a nasty surprise for the German troops invading the Soviet Union. The sloping armour offered good protection against most German weapons. The powerful long-barrelled 7.62cm F-34 gun proved to be a formidable weapon able to deal with all German tanks. The T-34 had a good power-to-weight ratio and wide tracks made it much more mobile than any other tank then in service. (Anderson)

and large parts of the country to the east were consigned to Poland and Czechoslovakia. In the west, the Saar region became part of France. Massive war reparations were to be paid by Germany in the form of coal, wood or food and other supplies. The army was limited to 100,000 men and any sophisticated weaponry such as tanks was forbidden.

In the prophetic words of Major General Foch of the French Army, "This is not peace, but an armistice for twenty years."

A majority of the German people felt this treaty to be an insult to the honour of the nation. Over the next decade many political parties were to use this underlying resentment to build a new political ideology. Consequently, the national parties quickly grew stronger and during this problematic time it was easy for Adolf Hitler to seize power. From this very moment violations of the Versailles Treaty were carried out more or less freely and without any consequences. By 1935, the first Panzer division had been formed.

The second was the unsuspected ease with which German forces were able to invade and conquer Poland and large parts of Western Europe in early 1941. The nationalistic fervour behind everything, the strategic and tactical skills of the military, and the Panzer force in the role of the impregnable spearheads appeared to underline Nazi propaganda…that Germany was superior!

The third was Operation *Barbarossa*, the invasion of Russia on 22 June 1941, which began promisingly but the ambitious strategic aims of the attack could not be achieved. Instead of reaching a proposed line from Archangelsk to Astrakhan, the German advance became stuck in the mud and snow of the harsh Russian winter.

A further problem for German forces on the Eastern Front was the appearance of an ever increasing number of modern Soviet-built tanks. Unnoticed by foreign nations, the underdeveloped Soviet Union had managed to design and develop two outstanding types of tank. The T-34 medium tank, based on the US-built Christie fast tank, had been in production since 1940 and was a revolutionary design which broke with all contemporary tank conventions. The hull had sloped armour providing enhanced protection and was fitted with a reliable 12-cylinder Model V-2 diesel engine. A powerful high-velocity 7.62cm F-34 tank gun was mounted in the turret.

The second tank was a heavy type. On first inspection the KV-1 appears to be of a more conventional design. However, as a heavy tank it was fitted with formidable armour protection combined with the same F-34 gun and diesel engine as fitted on the T-34. On each type, the engine and transmission was mounted in the rear of the hull, an ambitious technical solution, to save vital space inside the tank.

The sudden appearance of the T-34 and the KV-1 in the summer of 1941 came as a shock to German troops, who were to need all their tactical skills and the use of anti-aircraft guns such as the formidable 8.8cm FlaK as well as medium and heavy artillery to defeat this new threat. German infantry leaders for the first time encountered *Panzerschreck* (tank-shock). Troops became desperate after firing round after round at these heavy tanks without causing any damage. This desperation often led to a type of shock-induced panic, followed by a hopeless need to escape. Although this phase was soon overcome, the term *Panzerschreck* would not disappear completely.

German troops examine a KV-1 model 1939 in the summer of 1941. The turret has been hit 14 times by well-aimed 3.7cm or 5cm rounds, further impacts can be seen on the hull. None of the rounds penetrated the armour. In such a situation only determined action by close combat teams, or fire from the 8.8cm FlaK, could put this heavy tank out of action. The KV-1 mounts the 7.62cm Machanov L-11 gun. (Anderson)

Key data on German pre-war tanks

Type	Weight	Engine	Power/ weight ratio	Top speed	Ground pressure	Range on road	Range off road	Max. armour	Armament
PzKpfw I Ausf A	5.4t	Petrol, 60 hp	11.1	37 kp/h	0.39 kg/cm^2	140	93	13	two MG
PzKpfw II Ausf C	8.9t	Petrol, 140 hp	16	40 kp/h	0.73 kg/cm^2	190	126	14.5	2cm KwK, one MG
PzKpfw III Ausf E	19.5t	Petrol, 265 hp	13.6	67 kp/h	0.92 kg/cm^2	165	95	30	3.7cm KwK, two MG
PzKpfw IV Ausf B	18.5t	Petrol 265 hp	14.3	42 kp/h	0.77 kg/cm^2	210	130	30	7.5cm KwK, two MG

Key data on German experimental heavy tanks

Type	Manufacturer	Weight	Transmission	Performance	Top speed	Max. armour	
VK 30.01 (P)	Porsche	30t	Petrol-electric	2 x 210 hp	60 kp/h	50	?
VK 30.01 (H)	Henschel	30t	Petrol	300 hp	35 kp/h	60	?
VK 36.01 (H)	Henschel	36–40t	Petrol	550 hp	40 kp/h	100	?
VK 45.01 (P)	Porsche	59t	Petrol-electric	2 x 320 hp	35 kp/h	100	80
VK 45.01 (H) (Tiger Ausf E)	Henschel	57t	Petrol	650 hp	45 kp/h	100	100

Type	Range on road	Range off road	Ground pressure	Proposed main armament	Number produced
VK 30.01 (P)	?	?	0.9 kg/cm^2	7.5cm KwK L/24 or 10.5cm	one, hull only
VK 30.01 (H)	?	?	0.9 kg/cm^2	7.5cm KwK L/24	four
VK 36.01 (H)	?	?	0.9 kg/cm^2	Waffe 0725, taper-bore gun	one, hull only
VK 45.01 (P)	80	?	1.06 kg/cm^2	8.8cm KwK L/56	ten
VK 45.01 (H) (Tiger Ausf E)	100	60	1.04 kg/cm^2	8.8cm KwK L/56	1,346

Reinforcements became younger having been rushed through training and were poorly equipped to fight the ever-growing number of Soviet tanks. As morale deteriorated, the greater was the temptation to desert when facing a superior enemy force. Many archive documents detail that this complex problem was disputed by all levels of command. The approach of the general staff was simple: "The achievers of the German advance – captains and non-commissioned officers, should do what they were trained for – leading!"

German armoured forces in the 1930s

In the 1930s, the fledgling German armaments industry had developed a number of light and medium tanks. All the work was carried out under a cloak of great secrecy with each project given a code name.

The first tank to be produced in greater numbers was the LAS (*Landwirtschaftlicher Ackerschlepper* – agricultural tractor), later the PzKpfw I. Development of the vehicle began at the end of the 1920s, and resulted in a light tank armed with two machine guns and the typical layout of future German tanks – engine in the rear, driver and transmission in the front. The PzKpfw I was fitted with a turret mounting the main armament and also carried radio equipment, a significant feature at this time. This first mass-produced tank was used to establish a number of Panzer divisions, but was to be purposely used as the vehicle to train thousands of future tank crews. Germany was not motorized to a high degree (unlike the US military) but those mechanized units that did exist helped to train a large number of technically and tactically skilled personnel. In World War II, the tactical value of the PzKpfw I was very limited. However, it must not be forgotten that these tanks were developed under secrecy and with limited funding. The result was important, an operational tank which was available in substantial numbers.

The PzKpfw I was the first tank to be mass produced by Germany to equip the first Panzerdivisions and later it was used as a training vehicle. Armed with two Maschinengewehr 34 (MG 34) guns the type had armour only thick enough to protect the crew against small arms fire. Used extensively in the first two years of the war, the PzKpfw I had only a limited value in combat. The chassis of the PzKpfw I was used for a number of Selbstfahrlafette (self-propelled) guns. (Anderson)

The PzKpfw II was lightly armoured and mounted a 2cm KwK 30 cannon but was effectively used to attack and defeat enemy infantry positions. Although obsolete, it was still being used in 1944 as an escort tank in Panzer-Begleit-Kompanien (Tank Support Company) of the Heeres-StuG-Brigaden (Assault Gun Brigade). (Münch)

By early 1930, further light tanks had been ordered. One was to mount a 2cm *Kampfwagenkanone* 30 (2cm KwK 30) gun in combination with a machine gun. Developed under the designation LAS 100, it was later designated as the PzKpfw II and had a light amour hull designed to withstand light armour-piercing projectiles fired by infantry. When the PzKpfw II was used in action the design proved to be unsuitable for the intended role as a part of a *leichte Panzerkompanie* (light tank company).

The PzKpfw III was design as a *Zugführerwagen* (ZW – platoon leader vehicle) and was originally armed with a 3.7cm *Kampfwagenkanone* 36 (3.7cm KwK36) gun and three 7.92mm *Maschinengewehr* 34 (MG 34) machine guns. The vehicle was built using light amour plate intended to withstand only small arms fire. However, the PzKpfw III proved to be worthy of being uparmoured and upgunned. Later versions mounted a 5cm *Kampfwagenkanone* 39 L/60 (5cm KwK 39 L/60) gun, which made it an effective fighting vehicle.

The last mass-produced tank to be developed before outbreak of war was the *Begleitwagen* (BW – escort vehicle), which became the PzKpfw IV. Designed as a support tank, to control the battlefield, the PzKpfw IV mounted a 7.5cm KwK 37 L/24 gun, which fired effective high-explosive (HE) shells. The first versions were built with very light armour and as with the PzKpfw III the vehicle was progressively upgraded. The frontal armour on the PzKpfw IV Ausf A was 14.5mm thick, whereas on the final version the PzKpfw IV Ausf J this had been increased to 80mm. The PzKpfw IV entered production in 1937 and was still being built when the war ended in 1945.

The birth of the heavy tank

As mentioned earlier, the appearance on the battlefield of the T-34 medium and the KV-1 heavy tank certainly marked a turning point. Although the PzKpfw IV and the *Sturmgeschütz* III (StuG – assault gun) still had the potential to undergo upgrading programmes to improve combat efficiency, German military planners knew that the combat performance of these tank designs was limited. All future tank programmes were to be rigidly scrutinized.

By 1937, the *Heereswaffenamt* (Army Ordnance Bureau) had already given orders to develop a new tank in the 30-ton class with the companies Daimler-Benz, Henschel and MAN. By German standards of the late 1930s, these would have been designated as *schwere Panzer* – heavy tanks. At that time Nazi intelligence had become disturbed by the Char B1 (bis) and Char 2C heavy tanks in service with the French Army. These were the only contemporary heavy enemy tanks known to the German military as being ready for action.

A well loaded Panzer III Ausf J or L crossing a bridge in Russia, early 1942. (Tank Museum)

The PzKpfw IV was originally fitted with a short-barreled 7.5cm KwK L/24 gun. This low-velocity weapon lacked armour-piercing capabilities and accuracy over longer ranges. After the first engagements with Soviet T-34 and KV-1 tanks, a long-barreled version of the gun, the 7.5cm KwK 40 was quickly developed. With this gun the PzKpfw IV served until the end of the war. The PzKpfw IV shown is from 23.PzDiv (note the Eiffel tower marking under the tactical number 814). Although officially forbidden, the crew of this tank has mounted spare track links for added protection. (Wilhelm)

Designing a 30-ton tank

At the end of 1937, the first DW 1 (*Durchbruchswagen* – breakthrough tank) test vehicle had been completed and thoroughly tested. This was quickly followed by the DW 2 version. In 1939, Henschel delivered the VK 30.01 – the German military used a simple designation system, VK denoted *Vollkette* – fully-tracked and the first two digits denoted the weight class in metric tons, the last two the number of the test vehicle. The VK 30.01 test vehicle – a hull without a turret – followed proven German tank design principles with a rear-mounted engine and the transmission in the front of the hull. Frontal and rear armour plates were almost vertical and the superstructure did not overhang the hull side plates.

A PzKpfw V Panther Ausf A of II./SS-PzRgt "Wiking" passes through a Russian village in the spring of 1944. This medium tank was developed as the direct answer to the Soviet T-34 and broke with many traditions of German tank design. Fast and mobile, the Panther combined excellent armour protection with the powerful 7.5cm KwK 42 L/70 gun. Weighing 46 tons, it was heavier than a T-34 which weighed approximately 27 tons. (Anderson)

At approximately the same time, Professor Dr. Ferdinand Porsche received a development order for a heavy tank. As with the DW 1 and 2, a 7.5cm KwK L/24, the same gun as used on the PzKpfw IV and StuG III, was to be mounted in the turret. However, a suggestion was made to install a 10.5cm main gun.

The unsolved armament question kept the designers and engineers busy. In the early 1940s, a further type of gun was under discussion. Adolf Hitler, was keen on modern weaponry and demanded high armour penetration. He favoured a powerful gun with a low calibre; a large calibre gun would require more space in the turret and extra space for ammunition storage. The technology for such a gun with armour-piercing ammunition existed. Rheinmetall had worked on the 7.5cm *Panzerabwehrkanone* 41 (7.5cm PaK 41) with good results. The problem with the supply of special raw materials was to be a deciding factor. Tungsten in particular, essential to the manufacture of highly effective armour-piercing rounds, was available in very limited quantities. Two anti-tank (AT) guns designed to fire this ammunition were introduced, the 2.8cm *schwere Panzerbüchse* 41 (2.8cm sPzB 41) and the 7.5cm *Panzerabwehrkanone* 41 (7.5cm PaK 41). Only the PaK 41 was a success. However, the shortage of tungsten was so critical that these guns were never completely ready for action.

The VK 45.01 (P) was one of two design studies for a heavy tank. One team was headed by Ferdinand Porsche, who favoured a complex petrol-electric drive system. The other VK 36.01(H) was designed by Henschel and he chose to use a more conventional petrol engine and gearbox. Both designs were fitted with the same cylindrically-shaped turret mounting 8.8cm KwK 36 gun. (Tank Museum)

A pre-production PzKpfw VI Tiger (H) in the Henschel factory. The vehicle is fitted with an additional armour plate (not used on production tanks) which was lowered to provide extra protection for both the front plate and drive sprockets. The vehicle is still to be fitted with track guards and tools. (Tank Museum)

By the end of 1941, the first Porsche VK 30.01 (P) or *Typ* 100 test vehicle was ready. In mid-1941, it had been decided to mount a new type of gun, the 8.8cm KwK L/56 in the turret. This gun was to be manufactured by Krupp (as was the turret) and was developed from the formidable 8.8cm *Flugzeugabwehrkanone* (8.8cm FlaK).

Porsche, who was a brilliant engineer, chose to use an electric drive for the new tank. The power to operate the drive system was to be produced by using two air-cooled petrol engines to drive the generators. This technology was indeed very old but well-proven having been used on electric tramways, locomotives and some commercial vehicles. However, usage to power a tank capable of operating under extreme conditions was unknown territory.

In late 1941, new armour specifications were defined forcing Henschel to a complete redesign designated VK 36.01. The frontal armour protection was increased to 100mm from the proposed 80mm and it was intended to equip the tank with a taper-bore gun. The VK 36.01 was also fitted with improved running gear which had larger interleaved running wheels and no return roller.

The VK 36.01 was only an interim prototype. The final decision to mount the 8.8cm KwK L/56 in the Krupp turret led to a further redesign. The superstructure on the subsequent VK 45.01 (H) was widened to accept a larger turret ring. The tracks were widened to carry the increased weight of the vehicle. Despite the designation VK 45.01 (H), the tank weighed over 55 tons.

The designers and engineers at Porsche had to contend with the new specification for the armour. By May 1941, work on a new tank, the *Typ* 101 commenced. Unlike the VK 45.01 (H), which differed in almost every technical detail from the earlier VK 30.01 (H), the Porsche *Typ* 101 was based on the *Typ* 100. The armour was increased at the front from 50 to 100mm, the hull sides from 40 to 80mm and the rear plates were increased to 80mm. The performance of the two engines was boosted to 310hp and the transmission positioned in the rear of the hull. The rubber-tired road wheels were replaced by solid steel wheels and the return rollers were removed.

The decision

In early 1942, a decision to select which of the heavy tanks for production was not discussed. On the contrary, military planners established new units which should be issued with *schwere Panzer*. Interestingly, those units selected for deployment to North Africa (sPzAbt 501and 503) were to be equipped with the Porsche PzKpfw VI, surely because this tank had air-cooled power units. A third unit ready for establishment should receive the Henschel PzKpfw VI.

However, there was a certain discrepancy between the plans and reality. A letter from the *Panzerkommission* (Tank Commission) addressed to the Minister of Ordnance and Ammunitions dated 24 June 1942 reveals:

According to an official *Überblick* (a survey published monthly) dated 20 June, the planned production of PzKpfw VI Tiger was as follows:

Number 114 commanded by Alfred Rubbel of sPzAbt 503, during manoeuvres in May 1943 near the city of Karkov, in preparation for *Unternehmen Zitadelle* (Operation *Citadel*). Due to earlier combat experience, additional track links have been fixed to the front of the tank. Smaller improvements *Formänderungen* (modifications) were continuously incorporated and included a rain guard over the binocular telescope in the gun mantlet, fitted by the crews in the field. (Rubbel)

	PzKpfw Tiger (P)	PzKpfw Tiger (H)
June	---	---
July	12	15
August	12	10

Professor Porsche had no reservations regarding deliveries. Henschel stated delivery on the condition of solving the problem with the Argus Bremse steering mechanism until 10 July.

The *Panzerkommisssion* reported by 3 July 1942:

1. PzKpfw Tiger (H)
July:
The promised 15 vehicles cannot be delivered due to problems occurring with the gearbox, the steering unit and the brakes.
August:
At least ten vehicles will be delivered. It is very likely that the July deficit can be made up.

2. PzKpfw Tiger (P)
Due for delivery

PzKpfw VI Tiger "123" of sPzAbt 503, being replenished with ammunition. The 3-ton truck in the background carries the letter "M" (Munition – ammunition). A large indentation is visible below the cupola, an indication of heavy fighting. (Münch)

July 20	– two units
July 31	– eight units
August 10	– four units
August 20	– four units
August 31	– four units

Severe problems delayed the introduction of both the Henschel and the Porsche Tiger. By August 1942, only nine Henschel Tigers had been delivered and these were issued only to sPzAbt 502.

The continuous problems with the Porsche version led to the termination of the contract to build this vehicle and the Nibelungenwerk in St. Augustin, Austria had ceased production by August 1942. However Krupp, responsible for manufacturing the hull, had already completed the order.

By September 1942, Hitler demanded the production of a *schweres Sturmgeschütz* (heavy assault gun) based on the hull and running gear of the Porsche-built Tiger. Within a very short time the project had been thoroughly planned. In early 1943, the first vehicle was delivered and the last of the 91 vehicles ordered was ready for action in May 1943. These vehicles became famous under the name Ferdinand (the first name of Dr. Porsche). In 1943, after the surviving vehicles were returned to Germany to be rebuilt, the name *Elefant* (Elephant) was adopted.

The last Porsche-Tiger to be built was a *Befehlswagen* (command tank). In early 1944, and after a number of modifications the Befehls-Tiger was issued to *schwere Panzerjägerateilung* (sPzJgAbt 653), equipped with the *Elefant* tank destroyers on the Eastern Front.

The last note dealing with the Porsche-Tiger can be found in a collection of *Führervorträge* (lecture to the Führer), dated 4 November 1944. This interesting document, written under the impression of a totally lost war shows a lot of erratic statements. Every single paragraph starts with the words "the Führer demands":

> The Führer demands that the Porsche-Tiger, which are at present existent in the *Ersatzheer* (replacement training army), shall be combined in a company. These tanks, issued to different infantry divisions, shall serve as battering rams…

All of the Porsche-Tigers available at that time could not be driven over long distances due to continuing engine problems. The idea to get the vehicles into a fighting company and subsequently to spread the tanks over different infantry divisions without any support services shows a complete disregard of reality by Hitler and his cohorts.

Evolution – the Tiger B

While the Henschel Tiger Ausf E was being produced (1,346 units built), work on a successor had started. Hitler instructed Henschel to simply "improve" all components of the successful tank.

The armour plates of the new tank were sloped, creating a tank similar in appearance to the PzKpfw V Panther. The thickness of the frontal armour was significantly increased (from 100 to 150mm) but the side and rear plates of the hull remained at 80mm, but with an improved slope.

A longer gun, again derived from the 8.8cm FlaK 41, was to be installed. The 8.8cm KwK 43 L/71 was the most powerful tank gun available.

The weight of the new Tiger Ausf B increased to a massive 70 tons. The Maybach HL 250 P45 engine as used in the PzKpfw V Panther tank was used to power the 15 tons heavier vehicle. The reliable Olvar gearbox as used on the Tiger Ausf E was dropped, as it was thought not to be robust enough and a more conventional, but difficult to operate, transmission was installed. The result was a true heavy tank and comparable with the only other tank in this class, the Soviet-built JS-2. The latter was 20 tons lighter, but mounted a powerful 122mm D 25-T gun.

A total of 489 Tiger Ausf B was built. Quite naturally, Hitler still required advancements. Although the heavy tank had already exceeded all justifiable weight limits, a *schweres Sturmgeschütz* (heavy assault gun) was demanded. A massive 12.8cm PaK 80 L/55 gun was mounted in a fixed superstructure and the hull of the Tiger Ausf B had to be lengthened and the frontal armour increased to 250mm.

The first fifty PzKpfw VI Tiger B built by Henschel were fitted with the Porsche-designed turret as these had already been completed for the defunct VK 45.02 (P). The vehicle is not equipped with tools and recovery hawsers; track guards are not fitted and it is not coated with Zimmerit. This suggests that the tank is on trials at the Henschel Panzerversuchsstation (tank testing ground) in Haustenbeck. (Anderson)

Organization 2

In early 1942, the organizational framework for what would become a *schwere PanzerAbteilung* (sPzAbt – heavy tank battalion) evolved long before the first Tiger tank was built.

By 16 February 1942, two heavy tank companies had been established, initially without equipment, as detailed in this part of the *Kriegsgliederung* (Order of Battle).

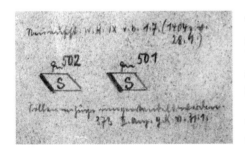

This excerpt of the *Kriegsgliederung des Feldheeres* May 1941 through May 1942 shows the newly established *schwere Panzer-Kompanie* (sPzKp) 501 and 502, to be ready for action by 1 July 1942. Changes in this order of battle were recorded handwritten. These core units had no tanks at all.

By 10 May 1942, *schwere PanzerAbteilung 501* (sPzAbt 501) had been established and the two independent heavy tank companies were immediately subordinated under this battalion. Some days later, sPzAbt 502 and 503 were formed and ordered to be ready for action. However, the heavy tanks were still not available.

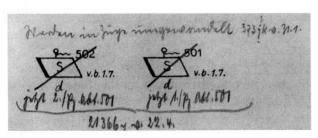

Only one week later the companies were officially disbanded and subordinated under sPzAbt 501. From this time the companies were listed as sPzKp.

The commander of a Befehlstiger from sPzAbt 503 gives a hand signal, certainly on the direction of a propaganda photographer. Other simple ways of communication used throughout the war included flares, signal batons and flags. Behind the officer is the "star"-type antenna for the Funksprechgerät 8 (Fu 8) radio set. The letter "I" denotes that the tank is from the signals echelon of the staff company. (Buchner)

This handwritten change to the *Kriegsgliederungen* shows the new sPzAbt 501, 502 and 503, units as battalion size. The sPzAbt 213 also detailed here was equipped with *Beutepanzer* – captured ex-French Army Char B1 (bis) heavy tanks. The unit was later transferred to the Channel Islands.

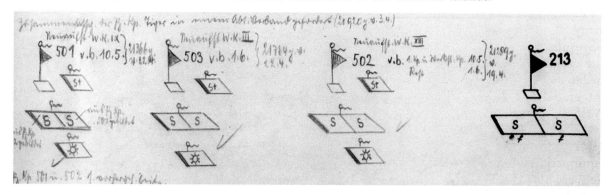

At that time it was planned to equip sPzAbt 501 and 503 with the PzKpfw VI (P). Both units were to be sent to North Africa, since the Porsche-built tanks had air-cooled engines which was thought to be an advantage in the hot desert conditions.

The sPzAbt 502 was to be issued with the Henschel PzKpfw VI (H) and it was planned for the unit to go into action on the East front.

The PzKpfw IV (P) proved to be ill-fated. Necessary changes to the engines and suspension forced the closure of all production. By October 1942, only ten tanks had been completed by Nibelungenwerke and these were used for trials, as well as for training the first Tiger crews.

The Henschel design, designated PzKpfw VI Tiger Ausf E (H) was selected to equip all Tiger units. However, production was slow. By August 1942, sPzAbt 502 deployed near Leningrad received only nine tanks. In North Africa, sPzAbt 501 was issued with 21 by the end of the year. The sPzAbt 503 were to receive 29.

Organizational structures

German military units were assembled in accordance to standardized organizational structures. The *Kriegsstärkenachweisung* (KStN – table of organization) involved the equipping the unit with vehicles, weapons and men. The *Kriegsausrüstungsnachweisung* (KAN – table of basic allowances) described basic requirements to be supplied to any unit. Since the latter included almost many items from typewriters to torches, it was far more comprehensive. For that reason, only detail from available KStN documents is used.

However, over time actual equipment changed due to new tables of organization being created. Heavy tank battalions in the field received reinforcements and new equipment only when necessary and, more importantly, when available. For this very reason, actual strength reports prepared by the staff for the higher command were not always correct. Often, surplus equipment was simply not reported and retained. A fine example was sPzAbt 505, which was allowed to retain some surviving PzKpfw III even after a new KStN had become valid.

PzKpfw VI tanks were regularly issued to battalion sized units on an army group level and were designated as *Schwere Kompanie* of PzRgt *"Grossdeutschland"*. This should be the standard organization, underlining the combat characteristics of the Tiger. However, there were exceptions. In late 1942, the first *schwere Tiger Kompanien* (heavy companies) were integrated into tank regiments. The first units to be equipped with the Tiger Ausf E in *schwere Kompanien* (sKp) were SS-PzRgt. 1 (five tanks in December 1942 plus four in January 1943) and SS-PzRgt. 2 (one tank in December 1942 plus nine in January 1943). Also by January 1943, SS-PzRgt. 3 was equipped with nine Tigers. *Abteilung* of PzRgt *"Grossdeutschland"* took delivery of seven Tigers and another two in February.

Initially, the first three sPzAbt 501, 502 and 503 not only had PzKpfw VI in their inventories, but also PzKpfw III, (see KStN 1150d and 1176d dated 15 August 1942). In the staff company, one PzKpfw III was used as a command tank (PzBefWg/SdKfz 268) by the ground-to-air liaison officer.

Photographed in the early summer of 1943, the crew of this Tiger from sKp/SS-PzRgt 1 "Leibstandarte Adolf Hitler" is cleaning the bore of the 8.8cm KwK 36 gun with a Rohrwischer (gun tube brush). Other than the Balkenkreuz (German cross) no further markings are visible. The tank is camouflaged with stripes (possibly olive green) painted over the standard dark yellow base colour. The smoke grenade dischargers have been removed from the sides of the turret. (NARA)

Schwere Panzerkompanie d

Theoretical organization structure according to KStN1176d dated 15 August 1942

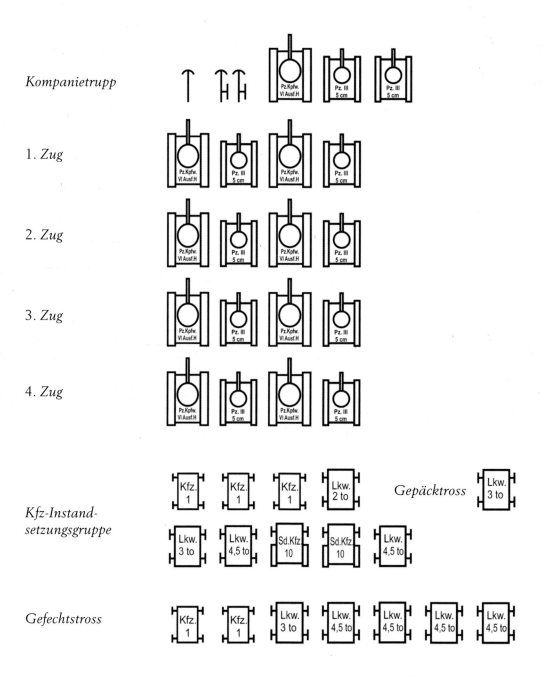

Another five PzKpfw III formed 1.Platoon *leichte Panzerzug* (light tank platoon) of the staff company and were mainly used for reconnaissance and communication duties. Furthermore, each combat company was equipped with ten PzKpfw III. The thinking behind this was to give the Tigers, if necessary, the assistance of light tanks in specific combat situations. All early sPzAbt were equipped with more PzKpfwg III (26) than PzKpfw VI Tigers (20).

It is obvious that the supply of vehicles to combat units depended on availability. As an example, if a *Typ 166 Schwimmwagen* was not available then another type of cross-country car would be delivered. Units, which were sent to the East received more *Maultier*-type tracked vehicles in place of standard 3-ton and $4^{1}/_{2}$-ton trucks. Again, the number being allocated depended on availability.

Both allocation of the light tank in a platoon and actual deployment were the responsibility of the commander of the *Abteilung*. If necessary, this would be changed to meet requirements.

The crew of this Tiger Ausf E from sPzAbt 505, attempt to conceal the tank under straw and foliage. The number "324" is painted on the side of the turret. A small tactical marking is visible next to the driver's visor which identifes it as a Tiger from 3rd Company. The tanks of sPzAbt 505 often carried tree trunks strapped to the sides of the hull. This vehicle has additional smoke grenade dischargers mounted on the hull. (NARA)

Stabskompanie d einer sPzAbt

Theoretical organization structure according to KStN1176d dated 15 August 1942

Kompanieführer
(Company commander)

Leichter Panzerzug
(Light tank platoon)

Nachrichtenzug
(Signal section)

Krad Erkundungszug
(Motorcycle recce
section

Pioneerzug
(Engineer platoon)

Fliegerabwehrzug
(AA platoon)

Instandsetzungsgruppe
(Workshop section)

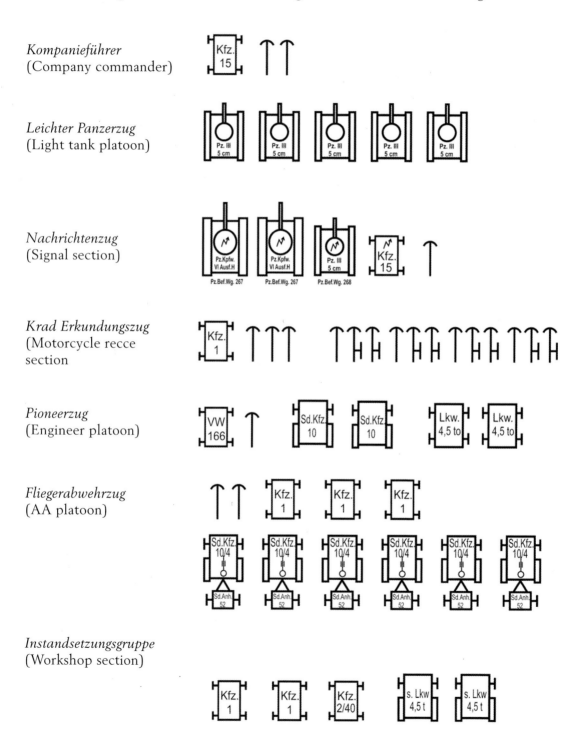

Verpflegungstrosse
(Ration supply train)

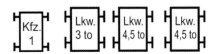

*Staffel Verwaitung
und Nachschub*
(Administration and
supply platoon)

Verpflegungstrosse
(Ration supply train)

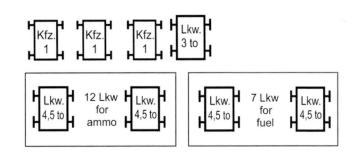

Sanitätstrupp
(Medical section)

Gefechtstrosse I
(Combat train I)

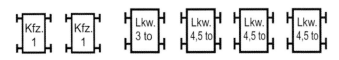

Gefechtstrosse II
(Combat train II)

A captured M4 A1 Sherman and a Tiger Ausf E from sPzAbt 504 with an SdKfz 169 Hornisse (Hornet) tank destroyer from sPzJgAbt 525 parked near a farmhouse in Italy. The 8.8cm PaK 43/1 L/71 mounted in the Hornisse was even more powerful than the gun on the Tiger. German units frequently made good use of captured Sherman tanks and many of these reliable vehicles were used for tank recovery duties. The mountains and undulating terrain of Italy caused the German tank forces many problems. When Tigers were driven over long distances, a great strain was put on the brakes, steering mechanism and the final drive in many tanks. After such journeys, only 40 to 50 per cent of the tanks would be ready for combat. (Münch)

The sPzAbt (heavy tank battalion)

The heavy tank battalion of 1942 equipped with 20 PzKpfw VI Tiger Ausf E and 26 PzKpfw III was structured as follows:
- *Stab* (headquarter)
- *Stabskompanie* (headquarters company)
- Two *schwere Panzerkompanien* (heavy tank companies)
- *Werkstattkompanie* (workshop company)

In early 1943, when a new KStN was written the companies were reorganized. All PzKpfw III were withdrawn and the number of PzKpfw VI per company increased to 14. Thus an *Abteilung* was considerably enlarged to three companies with a total of 45 heavy tanks and structured as follows:
- *Stab* (headquarter)
- *Stabskompanie* (headquarters company)
- Three *schwere Panzerkompanien* (heavy tank companies)
- *Werkstattkompanie* (workshop company)

In November 1943, the KStN was modified once again as 1150e and 1176e which were written to accommodate the PzKpfw VI Tiger B.

Kompanieführer (company commander)

The company commander was head of the unit and was issued with a cross-country car and motorcycles.

Stabskompanie (staff company) and Teileinheiten (sub-units)

The staff company comprised a number of basic elements, which were adapted to the needs of a battalion size unit. Very much like *Sturmgeschütz* units, sPzAbt

A Tiger Ausf E from sKp/SS-PzRgt 1 "Leibstandarte Adolf Hitler" on the vast steppe of central and southern Russia.
The turret number is stenciled in black outlined numerals on the side of the turret. The smoke grenade discharger mounting is in place but the discharger tubes have been removed by the crew. Although important for protection, the grenades could be ignited by enemy gunfire. A towing cable is connected to the front shackle, ready for recovery on the battlefield. (NARA)

were to be deployed as a concentrated force in combat. Contrary to this basic principle single Tiger companies were sent to pinpoint targets relying on the support of locally positioned units, that is if there were any.

leichte Panzerzug (light panzer platoon)

The light tank platoon was the original establishment used for a number of purposes, including scouting.

Major Lueder, commander of sPzAbt 501 summarized in his report *Tiger Erfahrungen in Tunesien* dated 18 March 1943 as follows:

> The differing losses of light and heavy tanks lead to steady changes to the organizational structure of the unit. Final conclusions based on recent experiences can currently not be given. It is however certain that the organic integration of light PzKpfw III in Tiger units must be basically maintained. Communication, reconnaissance, covering, mobility for the commander, transport of spare parts or recovery of wounded can only be solved by using light tanks. It is not sufficient to attach a light company to the *Abteilung* – each Tiger company commander must strictly have light tanks at his disposal at any time.
>
> It will depend on situation and terrain whether a light tank will be assigned to each Tiger, or if the company leader will commit them in combination.

In uncleared or mountainous terrain, which might be interspersed with enemy infantry, each Tiger needs a light tank for cover. In clear terrain only the Tiger must be ahead, the light tanks can remain in the rear at the disposal of the company commander. The hitherto existing structure of two Tigers and two light tanks per platoon can be retained for the time being...

Hauptmann Lange, commander of 2/sPzAbt 502 writes in an after action report dealing with combat by *Heeresgruppe Nord* (Army Group North) dated January 1943:

...Panzer VI and Panzer III must never be separated... Both PzKpfw III platoons can be deployed on reconnaissance duties at the front or on the flanks. They protect the PzKpfw VI against infantry anti-tank teams, and will be used in the attack against soft or area targets...

But:

...The provision with supply services, and new war strength report and war equipment information will have to be newly established after evaluation of the first after action reports...

The sPzAbt 503 reported in an after action report for the period of 2 to 22 February 1943:

22 February 1943
After the attack on Anastassijevska on 21 March 1943, which lasted until dark, the *Abteilung* lost two PzKpfw III (destroyed) and, due to strong resistance, used up all of its ammunition. The *Abteilung* now received orders to guard the bridges at the Ssarmatskaia cutting and south at Sovchose No.15.

For this task PzAbt 116 allocated one Platoon to the *Abteilung*. The total mission strength was:
   Two PzKpfw VI
   One PzKpfw IV (7.5cm Lang)
   Three PzKpfw III (5cm Lang)
   Five PzKpfw III (7.5cm Kurz)

This example shows that it was common practice to reinforce Tiger units with light tanks. The PzKpfw IV mentioned in this strength report was requisitioned from another unit.

However, during operations with a mixed establishment the PzKpfw III were attacked first, since these easy targets attracted the enemy fire.

Thus new KStNs (war strength report) were published already by March 1943. Any newly activated sPzAbt and all older units being under reorganization were to be organized according to the KStN 1150e and 1176e, both dated 5 March 1943.

Apparently it took time until all new regulations came into effect. In a teleprinter message dated 24 February 1942, the *Generalstab des Heeres* (General Staff of the Army) gave the following orders:

1) GenStdH orders:
a) any newly to be established sPzAbt Tiger (including sPAbt 506) has to be issued with three sPzKp (heavy tank companies) each.
b) for the sPzAbt 504, 501 and 505 one, for sPzAbt 502 two further sPzKp have to be established in this order (with a higher priority than 1a).

2) Formation:
a) Battalion staff: two PzKpfw Tiger
   Light platoon: six PzKpfw IV
b) Company: Headquarters two PzKpfw Tiger
               Two platoons each four PzKpfw Tiger

The escort tanks are to be withdrawn but, those already issued to existing sPzAbt will remain, but will not be replaced upon loss…

Apparently it was planned to withdraw the PzKpfw III *Begleitpanzer* (escort tanks), but to keep the light platoon, which was to be issued with PzKpfw IV. This matter remains mysterious, and cannot be solved at the moment.

A late production Tiger Ausf E from sPzAbt 507, with the turret number 223, near Warsaw on the Eastern Front in the autumn 1944. Among the numerous improvements introduced during the production run of the Tiger was a cast-steel shallow cupola on the turret. Steel running wheels were fitted to solve the problem with the earlier type, which frequently shed the rubber tyre. The move also saved on the usage of a vital commodity. (Anderson)

The crew of a Tiger Ausf E of 9.sKp/PzRgt "Grossdeutschland" during a break in operations deploying a large German flag over the turret to assist identification by patrolling aircraft from the Luftwaffe. The hand-painted winter camouflage has partly worn off. After sPzRgt "Grossdeutschland" was enlarged to three heavy tank companies, the tanks carried the identifiers A, B and C plus a two digit number on the sides of the turret. (Tank Museum)

The Panzer-Regiment "*Grossdeutschland*" reported on 15 April 1943:

> …The PzKpfw III in a Tiger – company

Employment has shown that the PzKpfw III, initially intended as a covering vehicle for a Tiger, is not able to withstand the enemy fire in the advance party. The enemy's anti-tank (AT) weapons attack the PzKpfw III first. With reference to the unit's combat readiness it seems to be favourable to keep only the company Tiger, since alone the entrainment of PzKpfw III spare parts beside the heavy Tiger spare parts requires a voluminous and complicated maintenance section. For this reason it is appropriate to restrict the Tiger units to one type – the PzKpfw VI.

The integration of a light tank platoon in a heavy tank battalion was not without controversy. The existence of two tank types within one unit implicated a number of challenges, if not problems. The workshop had to deal with two mechanical systems also spare parts and ammunition had to be provided. With enough Tigers at hand, new war strength reports were introduced.

Again from an after action report of PzRgt "*Grossdeutschland*" dated 27 April 1943:

> It is intended to reorganize each Tiger *Abteilung* with three companies. Each company has 14 Tigers. According to the war strength report the headquarters company will be issued with:
> a) One reconnaissance and cover party section of six PzKpfw IV (Lang)
> b) One armoured pioneer platoon

It has not been possible to confirm that the PzKpfw IV was officially issued to Tiger units. The reference in this report is possibly the result of a simple typing error.

Despite this clear date the Inspector General of Armoured Forces responded to the PzRgt "*Grossdeutschland*" after action report by 14 May 1943:

>...An establishment of Tiger units with PzKpfw III or IV is not regarded as necessary. Since Tiger *Abteilungen* must have reconnaissance elements, the Inspector General ordered formation of an experimental reconnaissance platoon (armoured half-tracks) for sPzAbt (Tiger) 503. According to the experiences made by sPzABt 503 the Inspector General will decide...

The *leichter Panzerzug* in the staff company and the light tank detachments in the companies were finally disbanded. For scouting, covering and all other associated duties SdKfz 250/1 and 250/5 half-track vehicles were issued. The designation was altered to *gepanzerter Aufklärungszug* (armoured reconnaissance platoon).

A report dated 28 May 1943, published by the Tiger training school at Paderborn again notes the use of the PzKpfw IV in a Tiger formation:

>...The advisable employment of smoke is executed too infrequently. According to the future provisioning of heavy tank battalion only the reconnaissance section of a unit (PzKpfw IV) will be able to fire smoke shells. For this reason development of smoke shells for the 8.8cm gun is urgent. The Tigers smoke dischargers are intended only for close concealment during disengagement from mine fields or during recovery missions under enemy observation...

Supply services, workshop and all other elements were adapted to the new structure.

Nachrichtenzug (signal platoon)

The *Nachrichtenzug* was originally issued with two *Panzerbefehlswagen* Tiger (PzBefWg – command tank) fitted for radio traffic within the *Abteilung* and equipped with powerful *Funksprechgerät* 6 and 8 (Fu 6 and Fu 8) radio sets. A PzBefWg III with Fu 6 and Fu 7 radio equipment was issued for use by the *Fliegerverbindungsoffizier* (ground-to-air liason officer). After withdrawing the PzBefWg III from the *Abteilungen*, a third PzBefWg Tiger was issued.

Krad-Erkunderzug (motorcycle reconnaissance section)

A small section originally used for reconnaissance and scouting. In 1943, after the introduction of the new KStN it was disbanded. Parts of the section's duties were incorporated into the *gepanzerter Aufklärungszug* (armoured reconnaissance platoon), other duties to the *Erkundungs-und Pionierzug* (scouting and pioneer platoon).

Pages 36/37
By May 1944, sPzAbt 503 was positioned in France to reinforce German defences. On arrival two companies were equipped with Tiger Ausf E, the other with the new Tiger Ausf B. The unit was one of many destroyed at the Falaise Pocket in August 1944. Surviving personnel were withdrawn to Germany, where the unit was reformed and equipped with the Tiger Ausf B. This late production Tiger Ausf E is fitted with steel-tyred running wheels and is coated with Zimmerit, a concrete-like paste, applied to protect against an attack with a magnetic mine. (Kadari)

A Tiger of sPzAbt 505 (note the tree trunks strapped to the side of the hull) on a temporary loading jetty ready to be ferried across a river. The transportation of a tank in this weight class over water could set pioneer and support troops many problems. The Tiger has received a heavy coat of camouflage over the standard dark yellow base colour. The smoke grenade dischargers have been removed but the mounting brackets remain in place. (Anderson)

Pionierzug (pioneer platoon)

The pioneer platoon fulfilled important tasks in the *Abteilung*. Originally it was equipped with soft-skinned vehicles only. With the new 1943 KStN the platoon's duties were expanded, as evident by the new designation *Erkundungs und Pionierzug* (scouting and pioneer platoon) and were equipped with the 2-ton *Maultier* (Mule) half-tracked trucks, a more appropriate vehicle for conditions on the Eastern Front. Later, a specialized version of the SdKfz 251/7 armoured half-track was introduced.

The General staff of the SS-PanzerKorps published the following experiences reported by the SS-PzGrenDiv *"Leibstandarte Adolf Hitler"*, SS-PzGrenDiv *"Das Reich"* and SS-PzGren Div *"Totenkopf"*:

The missions of the *Panzer-Pionier-Züge* (Tiger) can be broken down into three groups:

1) Scouting
2) Clearing of obstructions and obstacles of all kind. Road and bridge repair and strengthening.
3) Assistance in recovery of broken down tanks...

...The steady transport of building material for Tiger-bridging on heavy trucks to rapidly reinforce crossings is most important.

Disagreeing with the valid war strength report the SS-PanzerKorps demanded an increase in the number of vehicles:

> ...four *mittlere Pionier-Panzerwagen* (mPiPzWg SdKfz 251/7), four Porsche (VW) *Schwimmwagen*, three Opel *Maultier* trucks...

Fliegerabwehrzug (anti-aircraft platoon)

Originally the *Fliegerabwehrzug* was equipped with six SdKfz 10/4, light halftracks each mounting a 2cm FlaK 38 gun.

The 1943 KStN detailed many changes. The SdKfz 10/4 were replaced by three SdKfz 7/1, 8-ton halftracks each with a 2cm *Flakvierling* quadruple mounting, a significant increase in firepower.

Apparently not every unit received these mobile anti-aircraft guns. An after action report submitted by sPzAbt 503 dated 10 October 1943:

> ...The anti-aircraft (AA) platoon, which is still organized according the old KStN with six 2cm FlaK 38 guns, did perform excellently (seven confirmed kills). The essential factor for the AA platoon is the ability to protect the separate elements of the unit at different places. For this reason the *Abteilung* prefers to have six Flak 38 rather than three 2cm *Flakvierling*.

By late 1943, all existing self-propelled (SP) anti-aircraft weapons issued to tank units were felt to be obsolete in regard to mobility and armour protection. For this reason the chassis of the PzKpfw IV was chosen as the basis for the production of new anti-aircraft tanks. By June 1944, the *Möbelwagen* (Furniture Van), which mounted a 3.7cm FlaK 43 on a flat superstructure with fold-down side platforms was ready to be issued. In the new KStN 1176, eight *Möbelwagen* formed the new *Panzerfliegerabwehrzug*

On the Eastern front in early 1944, Pioneers have assembled a ferry from pontoons to transport a Tiger Ausf E from sPzAbt 506 over the Dniester (Dnjestar) river. Note a Maschinengehwehr 34 (MG 34) is mounted on the cupola for defence against any attack by enemy aircraft. A slow moving ferry loaded with a heavy tank provided an easy target. (Anderson)

(AA tank platoon). These vehicles lacked armour protection for the gun crew, especially during the attack. For this reason a new AA tank based on the PzKpfw IV chassis was developed. The *Wirbelwind* (Whirlwind) which mounted a 2cm *Flakvierling* 38 quadruple gun fitted in a nine-sided open-topped turret. The KStN was adapted for both new tank types and each platoon was issued with four *Wirbelwind* and four *Möbelwagen*.

In the autumn of 1944 and due to the limited number of vehicles available only sPzAbt 503, 506 and 509, and sSS-PzAbt 501 and 503 were issued with PzFla-Zug.

In this context, an essay published in January 1945 *Nachrictenblatt der Panzertruppen* is noteworthy:

…Attacks by enemy airplanes

1) The armoured forces and the air force are the mainstay of modern warfare. Due to their high mobility they are perfectly suited for close cooperation. On the other hand the enemy air force can be the most dangerous adversary for tanks by tactically skilled deployment of all types of weapon…

2) Armoured formations were attacked by warplanes during the advance and in assembly positions with explosive bombs. The "bomb-carpet" proved to be effective, but is uneconomic.

3) To effectively defeat tanks on the battlefield, it is necessary to attack each individual tank, a task, which cannot be solved by bombers. Light tanks can be destroyed by a fighter airplanes' weapons. Heavy tanks will only be damaged and total destruction is unlikely.

An attack by fighter-bombers with explosive bombs is not effective due to the low hit probability. Tanks can only be destroyed by a near or direct hit.

4) To effectively destroy heavy tanks the construction of specialized "tank hunters" is necessary. By the installation of heavy guns in single-engine aircraft these were able to destroy even heavy tanks. These tank hunters are called "tank-buster" by the enemy.

When the attack is carried out at low-level flight. Fire is opened first with machine guns (MG) and when the MGs are zeroed in, the guns will be fired…

5) The tank hunters are out-dated by the introduction of the rocket armed fighter-bomber, which presents the most sophisticated stage of this development…

…The rocket has, due to high velocity, a great penetration power. Thanks to its flat trajectory it has a high accuracy… The attack is carried out in low-level flight. The fire will be opened from ranges of 600 to 1,000m from the target. So far in the European theatre of war only British rocket-armed airplanes (usually only Typhoons) were operational.

A Tiger Ausf E from sPzAbt 503 climbs a steep bank to get back on the road. In combat, such a manoeuvre could prove to be fatal as the lightly-armoured underside of the tank is vulnerable to fire from enemy anti-tank weapons. The tank is fitted with a custom-built Gepäckkasten (turret basket). (Hoppe)

Pages 42/43
A Tiger Ausf E from an unknown unit is examined by German infantry. The tank crew has uparmoured the vehicle by placing spare track links on the front plate. (Anderson)

6) The advantages of air-based tank combat (high mobility and independence of the terrain) are accompanied by disadvantages:
a) lower speed than a fighter airplane
b) great dependence on weather and visual conditions
c) great susceptibility to ground-based defence (light AA guns, MGs and rifle fire).

7) The defence against the tank-buster demands:
Camouflage until completely hidden
Concentrated defensive fire with all weapons…

After the summer of 1944, when the army group center collapsed, the tactics for air-to-ground warfare by Soviet forces was confirmed. This extract from an article published in *Nachrichtenblatt der Panzertruppe*:

The (Soviet) air force introduced a new combat tactic – the pursuit

The purpose of the pursuit is the annihilation or destruction of
a) retreating enemy forces
b) heavy weapons and ammunition stores
c) the enemy railway network
d) supply lines and bridges, and the annihilation of counterattacks by the
   enemy air force…

The author placed special emphasis on the following combat principles:

…Reckless deployment at any weather condition, especially the Il-2 *Sturmovik* units, must be demanded.

The air raids must be enforced without interruption. The enemy must not get breathing time…

The Soviets relied on selective support for their ground forces – heavy artillery bombardment was deployed at almost any time and wherever possible. Evidently, it was not the Soviet tank force that inflicted devastating losses in German personnel and material, but the artillery. This is possibly one reason why the German basic principle of attack was applied even under most unfavorable conditions.

Instandsetzungstaffel und Bergegruppe (Maintenance and recovery section)

The original KStN dated August 1942, detailed only a relatively small workshop section intended to assist tank crews during routine maintenance. For serious problems the unit relied on the *Panzer-Werkstattkompanie* (workshop company), which was also part of the *Abteilung*. Parts of the smaller workshop section were changed in 1943. The number of vehicles allocated to the workshop company was doubled and because of the increase in transport capacity two cranes were issued. Furthermore, a recovery section was formed. However, the two *Bergeschlepper* 35t (recovery tanks) required to replace the four SdKfz 9 heavy half-track vehicles never materialized.

Sanitätstrupp (medical troop)

The medical troop was equipped with a cross-country ambulance car, a truck and an SdKfz 251/8 armoured half-track ambulance. This unit structure remained valid throughout Word War II.

Nachschubstaffel und Gefechtstross (supply and combat transport sections)

These important sections were equipped only with trucks. Only few changes were to take place over the time, generally the number of trucks used for transporting ammunition was increased from 12 to 16, and the number used to transport fuel was increased from seven to eight.

Panzerkompanie (tank company)

Initially, each sPzAbt had two companies each with 20 Tigers according to KStN 1150d and 1176d dated 15 August 1942 (see chart). In March 1943, a new KStN 1150e and 1176e were issued and now each Abteilung was issued with three companies. The number of platoons in the combat company was reduced from four to three. Each company was equipped with 14 tanks; the nominal strength for the *Abteilung* was 45 Tigers, a significant increase. It was important, that production of the PzKpfw VI Tiger improved by 1943 to make this possible.

Production of the PzKpfw VI Tiger Ausf E
1942	69
1943	550
1944	794

Schwere Panzerkompanie e

Theoretical organization structure according to KStN1176e dated 1 November 1943

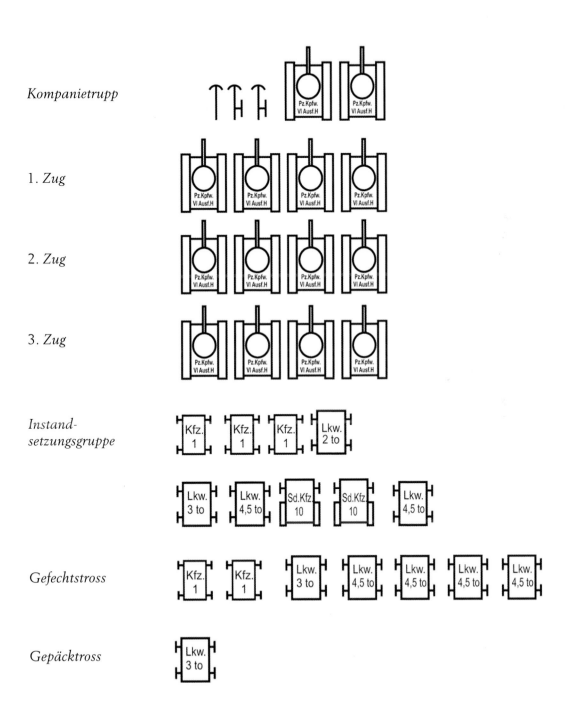

Kompanietrupp

1. Zug

2. Zug

3. Zug

*Instand-
setzungsgruppe*

Gefechtstross

Gepäcktross

Stabskompanie e einer sPzAbt

Theoretical organization structure according to KStN1150e dated 1 November 1943

Kompanieführer

Gerpanzerter Aufklärungzug

Nachrichtenzug

Erkundungs und Pioneerzug

Fliegerabwehrzug

Instandsetzungsgruppe

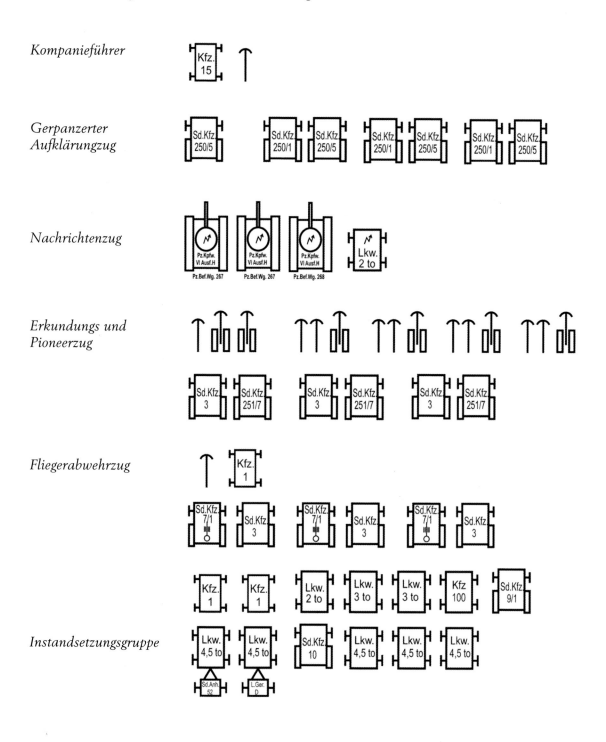

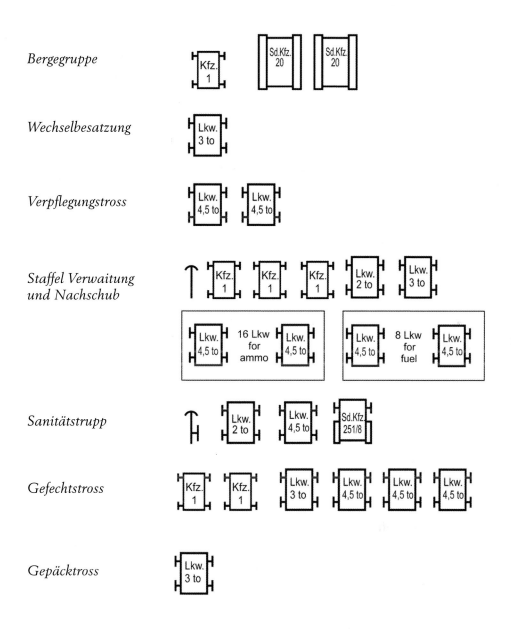

Bergegruppe

Wechselbesatzung

Verpflegungstross

Staffel Verwaitung und Nachschub

Sanitätstrupp

Gefechtstross

Gepäcktross

By November 1943, the KStNs 1150e (staff company) and 1176e (heavy tank company) were again adapted to cover the introduction into service of the new version of the PzKpfw VI Tiger Ausf B. The organizational structure now allowed the issue of either Tiger Ausf E or Tiger Ausf B to frontline units.

"freie Gliederung" (unrestricted)

By 1 June 1944, a new organizational structure, as detailed in a new KStN 1107fG, became valid and the *Stabskompanie* was extensively altered and effectively scaled down. The reconnaissance and pioneer platoon was equipped with five standard 3-ton trucks replacing three *Maultier* half-tracked trucks. The workshop platoon, the recovery section and all supply services including the medical troop were disbanded. The overall size of the headquarters company was thus reduced from 290 to 171 personnel.

The *schwere Panzerkompanie* (fG) was also decreased in number. While the allocation of tanks remained unchanged, all workshop and transport elements were disbanded and the number of personnel reduced from three Officers, 55 NCOs and 97 other ranks to four Officers, 45 NCOs and 38 other ranks.

The support services of headquarters company and all three heavy tank companies were passed to a new *Versorgungskompanie* (supply company) as detailed in KStN 1151b (fG). This involved the medical troop (without SdKfz 251/7 armoured ambulances) and the workshop (with a reduced number of half-tracked tractors). Importantly, equipment for the recovery section was improved by the authorization of five SdKfz 9 heavy half-tracked tractors and five Bergepanther recovery tanks.

The February 1945 issue Bulletin of the Armoured Forces noted:

> All KStN(fG) for Panzer, *Panzergrenadier* divisions and army battalions will be adapted according to combat experiences and to the general personnel and materiel situation, they will be published with date of issue 1 November 1944...

The reason for introducing the *"freie Gliederung"* was possibly to relieve staff and tank companies, allowing them to be flexible and more mobile. It is important to note that at the same time the general supply situation had considerably worsened.

Panzer-Bergekompanien (tank recovery companies)

The German army suffered from a serious shortage in the supply of *Zugmaschinen* (half-tracked tractors) which were the only vehicles available powerful enough to recover stranded or damaged vehicles from the battlefield. The *Zugmaschinen* were considered to be of vital importance and increasing numbers were required. When the Tiger heavy tanks entered service the situation became even more aggravated. The PzKpfw V Panther and the PzKpfw VI Tiger were simply too heavy and required three to five Famo heavy half-tracked tractors (the type was powerful, but lacked traction due to low vehicle weight) to be coupled for recovery operations. With early knowledge of this problem, it was planned that the recovery

section of each headquarters company was to be issued with two SdKfz 20 *Bergeschlepper* 35t. However, as this vehicle was never built each unit would be issued with four *schwere Zugmaschinen* 18t, SdKfz 9.

During the heavy fighting in the East many lightly damaged tanks were lost due to Panzer units being inadequately equipped for recovery duties. The OKH noted on 29 December 1943:

> In the East countless tanks are lost due to the shortage of recovery vehicles. For this reason we request the chief of armaments to increase production of tractors in the first quarter of 1944 as follows:
> 18t Zgkw to 150
> 12t Zgkw to 150
> *sWehrmachtschlepper* to 170...

For this reason, specialized *Panzer-Bergekompanien* were established and deployed at army and army group level. The complete equipment inventory was detailed in KStN 1189, dated 1 November 1943. The unit had two platoons each equipped with nine Zgkw 18t (SdKfz 9) and three 22t (SdAnh 116) flatbed trailers for the recovery of tanks up to the PzKpfw IV. The 3rd company was to have been issued with nine *Bergeschlepper* 35t (SdKfz 20) and two 65t (SdAnh 121) heavy flatbed trailers. The non-existence of the *Bergeschlepper* 35t was common knowledge, so the KStN contained some interesting footnotes:

> ...recovery should be by *Bergeschlepper* 35t (SdKfz 20), or T-34 or KV-1. If the recovery is carried out with *schwere Zugmaschinen* 18t (SdKfz 9), in place of the *Bergeschlepper* 35t then two sZgkw 18t (SdKfz 9) will be used...

The fact that captured T-34 and KV-1 tanks were used as an integral part of official German military organizational structures casts a telling light on the production ability of German industry.

A Befehlstiger S01 (command tank) from sKp/SS-PzRgt 2 with other vehicles from the unit, a PzKpfw III and a sPzFuWg SdKfz 263 8-rad (armoured radio car) during Operation *Citadel* in July 1943. While the Tiger is painted in standard dark yellow camouflaged with broad bands of olive green, the other vehicles are painted in original field (dark) grey. (NARA)

Kampfgruppen (combat teams)

Kampfgruppen were formed for a limited period. Normally, these combat teams were especially established to react to specific demands or to solve particular combat tasks. Weapons of all types were employed including tanks, infantry, and artillery guns. This tactical organization had been deployed during the 1940 *Blitzkrieg* on Western Europe with excellent results.

During the war of attrition on the Eastern Front, all *Kampfgruppen* were compulsorily established. Many units suffered severe losses making their combat value close to zero. The merging of divisions or battalions was a necessary measure.

A fine example of a combat team with Tiger tanks was the *Kampfgruppe Sander*. During the final days of the 6th Army at Stalingrad, 2/sPzAbt 503 was reinforced with two PzKpfw VI Tiger and 13 PzKpfw III from what remained of the battle-weary PzRgt 201 (23.PzDiv).

From a document detailing night attacks dated 1 August 1944.

…Night attacks with tank units or mixed combat groups are promising, enemy AT guns and artillery cannot open directed fire. Mixed combat teams have great chances of success. The following establishment proved to be successful:

10 – 14 tanks	One company
20 – 30 APC	One armoured infantry company and one armoured pioneer platoon…

Note: APC – armoured half-tracked vehicles, SdKfz 250 and SdKfz 251.

A PzKpfw VI Tiger Ausf E fitted with a Feifel air-cleaning system. The equipment was fitted for when the type was deployed to Tunisia in 1942. Production of the system ended in 1943. (Anderson).

An after action report from 13.PzDiv dated 13 January 1944 notes the mixed structure of combat teams:

> Experience regarding the structure and leading of 13.PzDiv combat teams due to the current difficult situation with equipment...
>
> The formation of the mixed battle group resulted from recent combat:
> One PzGrenBtl... elements of the PzAufkl *Batallion*...:
> 15 to 25 APC of all types
> One *Panzer-Kompanie*, at best a *Batallion*...:
> 10 to 15 PzKpfw III and PzKpfw IV (average)
> One *Sturmgeschütz-Batterie* (occasionally)
> 4 to 6 assault guns
> One *Panzerjäger-Kompanie* (Self-propelled, 7.5cm or 8.8cm)
> 4 to 10 guns
> One 2cm *Flak-Batterie* (Self-propelled)
> 3 – 5 guns
> One *Artillerie-Abteilung* (Self-propelled, 10.5cm and 15cm)
> 10 guns (maximum)...

The commander of a Tiger from sKp/SS-PzRgt 2 requests information from two infantrymen during Operation *Citadel*. The unit's famous "Mephisto" marking is stenciled on the side of the turret. The smoke grenade dischargers have been removed from the turret, while the hull-mounted dischargers remain in place. (NARA)

Mobility **3**

The forces of Nazi Germany conquered over half of Europe with weapons of only average quality. The French campaign was won on the ground and in the air by *Blitzkrieg* tactics – the combination of both arms decided many battles. German artillery, supported by Junkers Ju-87 Stuka dive-bombers of the *Luftwaffe* purposefully prepared the ground for the *Panzerwaffe* (Tank Army) to attack. In 1940, the Western allies had more tanks (including more heavy types) but British and French high commands were unable and apparently unwilling to change their tactical attitude. Where there was a young and determined leader operating near the front, the situation could be different. Colonel Charles De Gaulle commanding 4e Division *Cuirassée*, a keen advocate of tanks, led a counter-attack against a German tank force at Montcornet on 17 May 1940. The operation was successful, the German tanks forced to retreat to Caumont.

Another important factor was (and still is) the role of the tank crew, the quality of its training and morale.

Mobility

The engine and transmission for a tank have to be selected depending on the role for which it is designed and the planned combat weight of the type. A tank is a complex vehicle and it is not only engine power that influences mobility.

German medium tanks built between 1940 and 1942 had a power-to-weight ratio of 11 to 13PS/t. The PzKpfw III and IV were fitted with 40cm wide tracks provided a ground pressure of approximately 0.93 to 1kg/cm^2. As a comparison, a fully-equipped infantryman weighing 100kg (standing on both feet) exerts a ground pressure of 1.4kg/cm^2.

The Soviet T-34 performed much better being fitted with wide plate-type tracks had a ground pressure of 0.64kg/cm^2. Even the much heavier KV-1 tank had a ground pressure of only 0.70kg/cm^2.

After sPzAbt 503 was annihilated at Falaise, it was reorganized and equipped with Tiger Ausf B. In October 1944, the unit was sent to Budapest, Hungary as part of the force to counter the political crisis in the country. The sheer presence of the Tiger B in the streets of the city assisted the Fascists to seize power preventing Hungary from declaring an armistice with the Soviet Union. The turret number 200 denotes this as the tank of the leader of 2nd Company. (Münch)

The interleaved running wheels allowed the massive weight of the Tiger to be spread over a wide area which resulted in a very smooth ride creating a stable firing platform. However, any replacement of damaged inner wheels was very time consuming. In winter, frozen mud could easily block the suspension system and immobilize the tank. (Halbe)

The development of the PzKpfw VI Tiger dates back to the late 1930s. At that time two main battle tanks (MBT), the ZW (PzKpfw III) and BW (PzKpfw IV) had been fully developed and were in production. A heavier type was now requested, almost certainly to combat French heavy tanks, of which the Nazi intelligence had good knowledge. Russia was very remote at that time! And here however, German military intelligence failed almost completely, both the T-34 medium and KV heavy tanks had been ready for production since 1939.

General Layout

The Henschel VK 36.01 followed standard German tank design principles. By 1941 standards it was heavily armoured (modern Soviet tanks were still unknown). The original design relied on a 12-cylinder Maybach petrol engine, which would have provided the tank with a good power to weight ratio.

The proposed turret was to be fitted with a taper-bore gun with penetration performances according to the latest requirements (100mm at 1,000m range). However, such guns required tungsten, and this was in short supply – a serious strategic problem. The only gun available was the Rheinmetall 8.8 cm KwK 36 L/56, and it required a turret to be designed to accommodate the weapon. The new turret designed and manufactured by Krupp was too wide to fit on the relatively narrow hull of the VK 36.01 (H). As a consequence the hull had to be redesigned, the superstructure being widened to accommodate the larger mounting ring for the Krupp turret. The redesign of the hull allowed the strength of both front and rear armour to be increased. The increase in vehicle weight required the running gear to be redesigned and fitted with wider tracks. Combat weight was increased by some 10 tons. Thus the new tank, now designated VK 45.01 (H), reached a new weight class – 56 tons!

Far left
Engineers prepare to lower a Maybach HL 230 P 45 engine into the hull of a Tiger Ausf E on the production line at the Henschel factory, Kassel. The idler wheel is yet to be fitted and the running gear has not been assembled. (Halbe)

An impressive photograph taken during mobility trials at Paderborn tank proving grounds shows a Tiger Ausf E climbing a steep slope. This would have stressed the components of the drive train which would then be thoroughly examined by technicians for reports to be made. This is a late production Ausf E fitted with steel running wheels to save rubber. (Anderson)

Engine

The radical changes to the design required a more powerful engine to be fitted. The replacement chosen was the V-12 cylinder Maybach HL 210 P30 (HL – *Hochleistung* – high performance) petrol engine, with a maximum power output of 650PS (641hp/478kW).

The first vehicle running trials with the HL 210 showed that the engine had a tendency to overheat, which could cause it to seize or catch fire.

The engine cooling system proved to be a constant cause of concern. All components had problems, and these had to be solved by the designers and engineers at the manufacturers. The workshops on the battlefront, however, were forced to keep the Tigers running in all circumstances. In combat, a burst water hose could immobilize even the mighty Tiger tank.

The sPzAbt 501 reported in May 1943:

…Regarding the overheating engines, the HL 210 engine caused no troubles during the recent time. All occurring breakdowns resulted from the low quality of driver training. In several cases engine failures have to be put down to the

A Tiger Ausf E is used to demonstrate that trees are not an obstacle to a heavy tank. As long as not too many trunks accumulate under the hull, the tank will remain mobile. (Anderson)

missing remote engine thermometer. Five engines have reached more than 3,000km without essential failures. A good driver is essential for the successful deployment of the Tiger, he must have a good technical training and has to keep his nerve in critical situations…

The troop was able to learn how to solve mechanical problems. An extract from an after action report by 13.*Kompanie* (Tiger-Kp) of PzRgt "*Grossdeutschland*" dated 27 March 1943:

…Engine:
Upon disabling the crew compartment heating system, all Tiger tanks showed an average engine operating temperature of 60°C. This temperature is almost too low for the Maybach engine. From that point in time no further engine fires occurred, the removal of the heating system led to a better air cooling of the exhaust tubes. However, the engines need regular exhaustive control and thorough maintenance. After longer running darting flames 50cm high emerged at the exhaust pipes, conspicuous at night…

The fuel lines on the HL 210 engine also caused problems being manufactured from poor quality material which easily deformed and slipped from the connectors. In other cases the pipes became permeable allowing fuel to leak, a frequent cause of engine fires. The fact that when the tank first entered service, the engine bay fire extinguishing system did not work properly and this led to vehicle losses. Workshops in the field repaired these deficient components until the manufacturers solved the problem.

After 250 PzKpfw VI Tigers had been built a more powerful engine, the Maybach HL 230 P45 with a maximum output of 700PS (690hp/515kW) was installed The Supreme Command of the Army reported on 25 May 1943:

> …Starting with chassis number 250251, the new production PzKpfw VI Tiger will be fitted with the HL 230 engine. Its introduction will take place without sufficient testing. During commencement of the HL 230 production several constructional changes will have to be adopted.…

Transmission

The mounting of the steering unit and transmission with the engine in the back of the vehicle gave a number of clear advantages.

- Better utilization of available space resulting in a smaller hull and less weight.
- Good protection of these mechanical components against frontal fire.

Indeed, Germany had built tanks with this type of compact drive train, the *Grosstraktor* of the early 1930s and the few *Neubaufahrzeuge* built used this layout. Possibly the experience gained during that time was not good enough to proceed with this technology. The fact that no German wartime armoured vehicle adopted this layout reveals unsolved technical problems:

- The arrangement of mechanical levers over a length of 3 to 4m was complex, making any adjustment in combat almost impossible.
- Since regular maintenance was required, positioning the drive train close to the driver offers direct access from inside the vehicle, under armoured protection and even in combat

A platoon from sPzAbt 506, pass along a sunken road. The lead vehicle is a mid-production Tiger Ausf E fitted with the shallow cupola manufactured in cast steel. Each tank company was numbered consecutively from 1 to 14 and identified by the colour of the unit badge and the turret number. Staff – green, 1st company – white, 2nd company – red and 3rd company – yellow. (Anderson)

For these reasons all German tanks were built using this arrangement. However, in 1944 a PzKpfw IV was experimentally fitted with a rear-mounted hydraulically-powered drive train.

For usage in the VK 45.01 (H), Henschel installed the best available gearbox, the semi-automatic Maybach Olvar. Unlike all other contemporary German gearboxes, the Olvar allowed the driver to pre-select a gear then a hydraulic system would automatically operate the actual changing process. The Olvar gearbox was clearly superior in design and operation to all other transmissions then available in Germany and was adopted for use in the production Tiger Ausf E (H).

The Olvar transmission made driving almost comfortable. Drivers did only occasionally stall the engine. Due to the ease of gear shifting, acceleration was reputed to have been better than that of the much lighter PzKpfw V Panther tank, but average speed over rough terrain was slower. Far more important was the fact that the drivers found the Olvar to be very reliable.

The PzKpfw V Panther, commonly referred to as being the best main battle tank (MBT) of World War II, required a highly-competent driver to operate

A Tiger Ausf E advancing across open ground covered by an SdKfz 251 armoured half-track. Since tanks were vulnerable to anti-tank (AT) rifles and guns, Panzergrenadiere (motorized infantry) were vital for advancing, reconnaissance and attacking enemy infantry. The widespread use of Schützenpanzerwagen (armoured personal carriers) helped to reduce combat losses. (Anderson)

A Tiger Ausf E completely bogged-down in a mud hole. Prior evaluation of the battlefield and careful observation by the commander and driver during combat was essential to avoid such a situation. Although strictly forbidden, another Tiger is being used to facilitate a recovery. (Anderson)

the complicated manual gearbox. Many veterans remember that they hated driving the Panther under difficult conditions in unknown terrain. Some younger drivers suffered severe anxiety as they feared operating the Panther in combat. One of the many problems German field units suffered was that the supply of skilled tank drivers never did meet the demand. Fuel shortages and a lack of vehicles at tank driving schools made thorough training impossible.

The widespread opinion (on both sides) that the Tiger was cumbersome to drive seems to be partly unsustainable. An after action report of 13.Kp (Tiger-Kp) of PzRgt "*Grossdeutschland*" dated 27 March 1943 reveals:

Driving characteristics:
In one case two Tigers were ordered to chase three T-34 tanks at a range of 2km. Despite a light covering of snow and frozen ground it was not possible to catch up with the enemy tanks. In terms of agility the Tiger is definitely not inferior. Thanks to its good mobility the Tiger is a perfect lead vehicle. For such a heavy tank its acceleration is amazing, a valid asset while leading an advance party. Banks of soft snow as high as 1.3m causes no problem at all.

The sPzAbt 501 noted in Combat Report No.6 dated 3 May 1943:

...The most remarkable aspect of the recent combat was that the Tiger could still be deployed after covering a 400km run... This proved that the Tiger can easily keep pace with lighter tanks. Nobody expected this....

As early as 26 January 1943, sPzAbt 502 prepared a bulletin for the high command of *Heeresgruppe Nord* (Army Group North) detailing a number of technical problems, which arose during the first deployments and proposed some technical changes.

Erfahrungsaustausch PzKfw VI Tiger
1. ...heating of the fighting compartment does not work properly, since
    a) ...warm air bled into the fighting compartment contained carbon monoxide.
    b) ...heating is not sufficient.
Corrective:
    a) Prevention by modified and additional seals...
    b) Sealing of warming hood has to be refined. Temperature of radiator fluid must be held at around 80 – 90°C. The bore of the water pipes should be increased...

2. Dismantling the gearbox leads to damage on the telescopic drive-shafts.
    Corrective:
    While removing the gearbox, the drive-shafts have to be removed and properly moved to the sides...

3. Absence of any attachment points at front and rear for the vehicle jack.
    Corrective:
    In future the attachment points will be enlarged.

5. The front torsion bars arm tend to bend under load, consequently forcing the outer road wheels to damage the inner wheels.
    Corrective:
    The basic material of the torsion bars will be improved. When extraordinary stress due to rough terrain (tree trunks, rock fragments etc.) occurs, the front outer wheels should be removed.

6. Loosening of the road wheel rubber tyres especially on the inner wheels.
    Corrective:
    The camber of the torsion bar arms must be increased.

7. Driver's visor clamps freezing
    Corrective:
    When frozen, rinse with Glysantin (anti-freeze liquid). In summer, do not oil or grease the parts.

A Tiger Ausf E of sPzAbt 503 bogged-down on marshy terrain. Any recovery would have to be executed by using the winches of several halftracks. If the recovery failed, the crew would have to destroy the tank by using two demolition charges: one placed inside the gun, the other in the engine bay. (Anderson)

11. Great expenditure of time for exchange of torsion bars (3 to 4 days)
Corrective:
Time consuming road wheel assembly can be alleviated by the use of special tools. Production of such tools is now underway.

14. Leaking final drives
Corrective:
The latest final drives are effectively sealed. New parts can be requested...

17. Track climbing over the drive sprocket.
Corrective:
Adjust the sprocket gear backlash. When wear damage is visible, the sprocket tooth rim has to be replaced.

24. Fuel feed pipes at the carburetor's leak.
Corrective:
The fuel pipes have to be checked frequently, all hose fittings must be tightened frequently. Future production vehicles are fitted with reinforced fuel pipes.

25. Visibility at night of exhaust gases and red hot silencers.
Corrective:
Exhaust covers and silencer deflector sheets will be supplied later.

These shortcomings occurred as a consequence of the rapid development of the PzKpfw VI Tiger. The test phase was apparently also inadequate. As a result, the first combat deployment came with a number of risks and since there was no other choice, these had to be accepted.

Careful evaluation of the many after action reports and numerous dialogues with crews showed that the transmission, in particular the gearbox system, was better that the perceived reputation. It simply required a good deal of care and precaution when operating in combat. In the hands of a good and responsible driver, and maintained by skilled engineers it worked.

However, there was a saying among the Tiger drivers: "Never, never try to steer while driving backwards". The Tiger Ausf E had a tendency to throw the track at the drive sprocket when reversing to the left or right. In combat this could lead not only to the loss of a track, possibly the tank and perhaps the crew.

Mobility in winter

The winter weather brought new problems. For more than six months of the year, combat on the Eastern Front was affected by weather conditions. September and October brought rain to such an extent that the whole of the country turned into a muddy hell. Only very good roads, and of course the railway system could guarantee a minimum of mobility (while tanks retained a limited degree of mobility, all supply trucks became stuck). The onset of winter brought very low temperatures, opening new challenges for both men and equipment. Furthermore, the Russian climate tended to show nasty up and downs, a sudden temperature rise in February could turn the firm road of yesterday into a sea of mud within some hours. A few days later the temperature could plummet leaving the heavily-rutted roads frozen solid.

A PzKpfw Ausf B Tiger, being driven towards advancing enemy armour during the spring of 1945. The Panzer group is supported by Panzergrenadiere in an SdKfz 251/9 armoured half-track vehicle armed with a 7.5cm KwK gun. (Anderson)

A battle-worn Tiger Ausf E from an unidentified unit is being replenished from a Maultier (Mule) half-tracked truck. The mobility of the tank force was reliant on regular supplies of fuel, engine oil and the delivery of spare parts. The track covers are damaged, the front mudflaps are missing. Note that areas of the Zimmerit-coating have been chipped-off, possibly due to enemy fire. (Münch)

The commander of the workshop of sPzAbt 502 wrote in a short after action report dated 14 April 1943:

Winter mobility of the PzKpfw VI is not favourable. The ice cleats supplied so far increase the tracks grip and avoid side sliding to a certain degree (as long as they are not fully worn). They do not meet the troops' demands, since the tracks tend to totally slip on slight slopes in icy terrain. The ice cleats get lost easily, the wear and tear is considerable (after 30 to 40km). The exchange of lost ice cleats on the march is difficult, since the respective track links have to be de-iced with a blowtorch. It is requested to deliver winter tracks with strong cast-on noses and sharp fins (40 to 50mm high) instead of single replaceable ice cleats. They should work in both directions. Ten to 14 winter track links could be inserted in each track. It seems to be certain that such winter tracks would guarantee excellent mobility.

Using tracks with ice cleats, the speed had to be reduced on hard frozen ground, since the strain inflicted to torsion bars and shafts is considerable. Apart from these shortcomings no further problems have occurred during the past winter, the tank totally fulfilled the requirements…

By autumn of 1943, new tracks with ice cleats on the treads were introduced. Sadly, there are no field reports available.

Tiger Ausf B

The PzKpfw VI Tiger Ausf B combined the assets of the Ausf E with the latest in German tank technology. The most obvious change was the use of sloping armour on the front of the hull, following the design of the PzKpfw V Panther medium tank. The thick armour protection of the Tiger E was exceeded and a new long-barreled gun was installed and this resulted in the weight of the tank being increased by some 15 tons.

The Tiger Ausf B was fitted with the same engine as in the PzKpfw V Panther, possibly to simplify supply as the engine was interchangeable. A new Maybach engine with a much improved power output was under development.

The Tiger Ausf E used the Maybach Olvar gearbox and there were many attempts on the part of the army ordnance bureau to adopt this excellent gearbox for the Panther, and certainly for the Tiger Ausf B. It was, however, decided to install the less complicated manual gearbox. This required skilled drivers able to handle the tank in every situation without faults.

On paper the Tiger Ausf B reached a top speed of 41.5kph/26mph and no data is available for acceleration and handling characteristics. However, it appears that vehicle mobility did not exceed that of the Tiger Ausf E.

Pages 66/67
October 1944, a Tiger Ausf B of sPzAbt 503 is positioned on a street in the city of Budapest, Hungary. The Tiger is fitted with the Henschel turret mounting the 8.8cm KwK 43 L/71 with a two-piece barrel. The turret shape was ballistically improved with no bullet traps. (Münch)

Below
Three of 14 Tigers Ausf B of 3/sPzAbt 503 issued to the unit in July, 1944 are lined up ready for training with live ammunition. This early production Ausf B is fitted with the Porsche-designed turret mounting the 8.8cm KwK 43 fitted with a one-piece gun barrel. (Münch)

Rail transport

The Sonderverlade-
Kopframpe (transportable
end-loading platform)
also known as the
"Tigerrampe" was used
for loading and unloading
Tiger tanks. (Kadari)

German armoured forces relied on rail transport wherever possible. This
was in part a consequence due the limited reliability of tank automotive
components and any needless wear was to be avoided. Important, too, was
the lack of an efficient road network on the Eastern Front.

The weight and dimensions (overall width in particular) of the Tiger was
a problem for the rail system.

Type SSyms railway cars (six-axle) were used to transport both the
Tiger Ausf E and Ausf B. The tanks, however, proved to be too wide to fit
the standard loading gauge and for this reason two types of tracks were

used. The normal combat tracks of the Tiger E were 725mm wide. For rail transport these tracks were to be removed and preplaced by 520mm wide transport tracks. The outer running wheels had to be removed from the suspension and this operation required 30 minutes per side to complete under normal conditions.

The Tiger Ausf B used combat tracks 800mm wide and transport tracks of 660mm wide. Since the layout of the running gear was different, the outer running wheels did not have to be removed.

The *Verladeketten* (transport tracks) were permanently carried on SSyms wagons. The transport troop was responsible for cleaning, maintaining and loading the tracks onto the wagon after usage.

The commander of sPzAbt 506 noted in his preliminary after action report dated 30 September 1943:

> ...I.) Rail transport
> The *Abteilung* was loaded on 11 transports trains over a three-day period between 17:00 on 9 September 1943, until 18:00 on 12 September 1943, using one *Sonderverlade-Kopframpe* (transportable end-loading platform) and one side-loading platform.
> In Snamenka, 25km northeast of Kirove, the transition from transport tracks to combat tracks should take place. This "way we planned to speed up unloading of the *Abteilung* at the destination, we estimated approximately 30 minutes per train. The trains, however, were redirected via Dnjepropetrovsk – Sinelnikovo to Saporoshje, which lacked loading facilities. There we had to use a poor quality

The Tiger units practised loading and unloading under most difficult conditions. A Tiger Ausf E from sSS-PzAbt 103 (503) slowly mounts an SSyms wagon using a ramp constructed from straw bales reinforced with the Tiger combat tracks. The Tiger is a late production Ausf E fitted with steel running wheels and a cast cupola. (Kothe)

Far left
The transportable ramp could be dismounted and loaded on the train ready for use at the destination. Here a "Tigerrampe" is fitted to an SSyms railway wagon ready for loading. (Anderson)

Two sZgKw 18t (SdKfz 9) haul an immobilized Tiger Ausf E from sPzAbt 505 on to an SSyms railway wagon. A third SdKfz 9 mounted with a 3-ton capacity Drehkran (rotary crane) pushes the heavy tank. The tank is fitted with a rain cover over the cupola. (Anderson)

and damaged end-loading platform, which delayed unloading significantly. For this reason the trains, which arrived quickly one after another, had to wait for $1\frac{1}{2}$ days...

...As late as 10 September 1943 the last transport was unloaded. The transport tracks were left on to expedite the transport of the Tigers to the front, where they were urgently needed...

This report shows that transport of entire units uncovered a lot of problems, and took a lengthy period of time to complete. The quality of the railway line, bridges and the availability of loading facilities often forced the transport troops to improvise.

By 15 January 1944, the commander of sPzAbt 506 wrote a report of experiences from 20 September 1943 to 10 January 1944 in the combat area north of Krivoj Rog:

...In the period from 20 September 1943 to 10 January 1944 the *Abteilung* has destroyed 213 tanks and 194 anti-tank (AT) guns and other artillery. The *Abteilung* fought alongside the following divisions:

9.Pz Div
123.InfDiv
16.PzGrenDiv
23.PzDiv
11.PzDiv
13.PzDiv
17.PzDiv...

Above

Although strictly forbidden in order not to endanger oncoming rail traffic, Tiger "224" is loaded complete with wide combat tracks; a frequent occurrence. The tactical number on the Tigers of sPzAbt 505 was stencilled on the gun barrel rather than on the side of the turret. Almost all tanks carried tree trunks strapped to the side of the hull. Note the small stock of track pins carried on the front of the superstructure. (Anderson)

Left

A freight train transporting Tiger tanks lies in ruins after an attack by aircraft or mobile artillery. (Erdmann)

Transport

The transfer via train encounters problems every time, because there are never sufficient SSyms wagons at hand. During the transfer from 29 and 30 December 1943, 13 Tigers departed. Three Tigers ready for action in Nikolajev and a further three in Krivoj Rog could not be picked up due to absence of SSyms wagons. Only by now (9 January 1944), did the *Heeresgruppe* manage to organize the transfer of 12 Tigers, which were repaired ready for action, from the Krivoj Rog/Nikolajev area, to the *Abteilung*. We count on their arrival by 20 January 1944.

Partisans were a further threat. Alfred Rubbel of sPzAbt 503 noted in his diary:

> …Because Russian railway bridges often had insufficient capacity, three *Schutzwagen* (protective wagon – empty railway cars) had to be coupled between each two SSyms Tiger wagons in order not to overload the railway track. Thus the great load was spread. Our train had five SSyms and 12 *Schutzwagen*. Wherever we had to fear partisans, two further *Schutzwagen* were coupled in front of the locomotive because of mines…

The SSyms wagons had to be requested in time. The transport tracks of the Tiger tanks belonged to the wagons and since Tiger Ausf E and Ausf B had different

A Tiger Ausf E, probably from sPzAbt 506, is loaded on an SSyms wagon. The tank is fitted with narrow transport tracks, which are chocked front and rear for safety. The wider combat tracks are stored under the tank. A Machinengewehr 34 (MG 34) is mounted on the cupola for air defence. (Anderson)

running gear, the transport tracks differed. The Bulletin of the *Panzertruppe* published a note on this matter in the September 1944 issue:

> The PzKpfw Tiger I and Tiger B have different running wheels and therefore need different transport tracks. These have to be marked with colour:
> Tiger I = Transport tracks with a coat of green paint
> Tiger B = Transport tracks with a coat of red paint
>
> Upon request of SSyms wagons for transport of Tiger it has to be noted:
> a) SSyms green = Syms-wagon with green transport tracks for Tiger I
> a) SSyms red = SSyms-wagon with red transport tracks for Tiger B
>
> The transport tracks have to be handled with care. Their coat of paint has to be preserved and, if necessary, renewed. After unloading of the tank the tracks have to be packed back on the wagon.

In conclusion, it must be stated that the German railway transport authorities did a very good job. The fact that most railway transports in the East arrived at their destinations is a sign of target-orientated management. In the West, the Allied forces made use of their air superiority and any transport of reinforcements or supplies by rail or road had to be carried out at night.

Firepower 4

PzKpfw VI Tiger Ausf E

The fearsome reputation of the Tiger Ausf E was based primarily on the firepower of the 8.8cm KwK 36 gun. Between the years 1942 and 1943, many stories circulated on both sides during the conflict and propaganda enhanced these tales, regardless of whether they were true, exaggerated or just fables.

As noted earlier, the decision to use the 8.8cm KwK 36 was made because the advanced taper-bore technology could not be introduced into production due to the precarious supply of tungsten metal.

The 8.8cm KwK 36 L/56 was a derivative of the renowned 8.8cm FlaK, making it the most powerful gun to be mounted in a tank. It had a barrel length of 4.93m (L/56) and the higher muzzle velocity of the armour-piercing (AP) round allowed enemy tanks to be attacked at long range. Thanks to this large calibre, a high-explosive (HE) round also had a devastating impact on the target.

Sighting devices

The first Tiger Ausf E were fitted with a *Turmzielfernrohr 9b* (TZF 9b) binocular sighting telescope which was used with the gun for ranges up to 4,000m and with the coaxial *Maschinengewehr 34* (MG 34) for ranges up to 1,200m.

It was thought that the performance of the binocular sighting telescope could be enhanced by fitting an *Entfernungsmesser 09* (EM 09) stereoscopic rangefinder. It is unclear how exactly this rangefinder should be used in combat and quite certainly it was not possible to install and operate the device from inside the turret. Major Lueder, commander of sPzAbt 501 comments in a letter to the Army Ordnance Bureau:

A Tiger Ausf E from sPzAbt 502 on a training exercise. The tank is armed with the powerful 8.8cm Kampfwagenkanone 36 L/56 (8.8cm KwK 36 L/56) developed from the feared 8.8cm Flugzeugabwehrkanone (8.8cm FlaK) and was one of the best tank guns of World War II. (Münch)

A Tiger Ausf E of sPzAbt 505 with the tactical number 313 is resupplied with ammunition during the summer of 1943. To facilitate loading, the crew have made a ladder from locally available materials. An attempt has been made by the crew to camouflage the tank with straw to conceal the huge tank in the vast openess of the Russian steppe. (Anderson)

The EM 09 problem:

…we received some EM 09 only recently, while the majority of the devices are still in Italy… We will have to find a number of men able to see stereoscopically. I see problems finding the medics needed for this procedure… This will take some weeks, and a great deal of work. The *Abteilung* is spread over some 250km and I cannot gather qualified persons under these conditions, and therefore unable to assign personnel for a course of instructions under these conditions. It is "war" here, and we have got better things to do… Practically the EM 09 will have to be handled from a person outside the tank…

Ammunition

The ammunition for the 8.8cm KwK 36 was derived from that designed for the 8.8cm FlaK gun, the ballistic performances being identical. However, the ammunition was not interchangeable. While the 8.8cm FlaK was fired mechanically using a percussion primer, the tank gun used an electric primer for firing.

The 8.8cm *Sprenggranat-Patrone* (SprGrPatr), high-explosive (HE) shell, could be fired with or without delay fuse.

The *Panzergranat-Patrone* 39 (PzGrPatr 39), armour-piercing (AP) shell was standard ammunition. This was often referred to as the *Panzergranate* or *Panzer-Kopfgranate*.

The reliable supply of ammunition was vital for any unit in the field and was transported to the tanks by any available vehicle. The Tiger had five escape hatches, one for each crew member and were designed to keep personnel losses to a minimum. All crew members of a JS-2 (including the driver) had to leave the tank through the turret hatch. (Münch)

The PzGrPatr 40 was a *Hartkern* shell, a tungsten high-velocity armour-piercing (HVAP) round which had an outstanding performance.

The GrPatr 39 HL (HL – *Hohlladung*, shaped charge) a high-explosive anti-tank (HEAT) round for use against tanks.

An official document published by *Oberkommando des Heeres* (OKH – Army Supreme Command) dated 1 April 1943 details the ballistic data for the AP ammunition.

Range:	100m	500m	1,000m	1,500m	2,000m
8.8cm PzGrPatr 39	118	111	100	92	84
8.8cm PzGrPatr 40	170	158	140	n/a	110
8.8cm GrPatr 39 HL	90	90	90	90	90

The superiority of the PzGrPatr 40 is obvious. The tungsten core shell was developed for many AT and tank guns of different calibres, but due to the general shortage of this metal there were never great stocks of this ammunition available. Sadly, the list gives no indication of the number produced or planned ammunition production for the respective 8.8cm shell types. However, for the 7.5cm KwK 40 the numbers are available. By December 1942, some 276,000 "standard" 7.5cm PzGrPatr 39 shells were available (with a further 135,000 to be produced in December), but there were no 7.5cm PzGrPatr 40 available at all (with only 5,000 to be produced in December). It is not known whether these carefully planned production targets were reached.

The *Waffenamt* compiled a list of the number of rounds which had been fired by April 1943. During the period December 1942 to March 1943, some 16,400 HE rounds were fired, also 19,000 PzGrPatr 39 AP shots, but only 100 PzGrPatr 40 were consumed, approximately 0.5 per cent of the total.

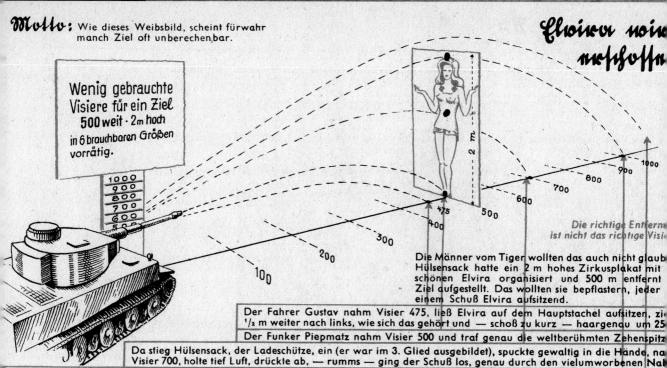

Der Fahrer Gustav nahm Visier 475, ließ Elvira auf dem Hauptstachel aufsitzen, zie... ½ m weiter nach links, wie sich das gehört und — schoß zu kurz — haargenau um 25...

Der Funker Piepmatz nahm Visier 500 und traf genau die weltberühmten Zehenspitz...

Da stieg Hülsensack, der Ladeschütze, ein (er war im 3. Glied ausgebildet), spuckte gewaltig in die Hände, na... Visier 700, holte tief Luft, drückte ab, — rumms — ging der Schuß los, genau durch den vielumworbenen Na...

Der Richtschütze Holzauge schüttelte den Kopf, denn bei Visier 700 hätte der Schuß doch drübergehen müssen. Er ging jetzt c... Ganze, nahm Visier 1000 und traf den Kopf.

Der Panzerführer Schnellmerker nahm Visier 1100 und schoß drüberweg. Mit diesem Visier war der Zauber also zu Ende.

Visier 25 m zu kurz, kein Treffer! Visier 500 m zu weit, Treffer! ! ! ! ! !

Da staunt der Laie, der Fachmann aber lächelt!

Moral: Die richt'ge Schätzung bringt gar nicht auch den Treffer, den man ho...

A page from the famous Tiger-Fibel, an attempt to teach young tank crews how to operate the tank by humorous means. It used many drawings of sparsely clothed females to draw attention to important operational data. This illustration deals with the exact adjustment of the gun sight. The Motto reads: Like this temptress, any objective appears attainable. Moral reads: Any estimation, even if thought true, will not lead to the desired success. (Anderson)

No figures are available regarding the PzGrPatr 39 HL. The same document reveals that figures for the 7.5cm PaK 40 and PaK 38 showed the percentage of *Hartkern* AP shells consumed as 23 and 21 per cent respectively.

Apparently the performance of the 8.8cm PzGrPatr 39 was considered to be adequate, explaining the low number of *Hartkern* shells produced. In mid-1943, production of *Hartkern* ammunition was cancelled.

Alfred Rubbel, a veteran of sPzAbt 503, remembers that his unit never suffered any ammunition shortages:

> If the supply was low, we tankers helped ourselves from stocks of *Luftwaffe* and *Heeresflak* units. Although the primers for the 8.8cm FlaK ammunition were different, we had learned to change them. The wise Tiger tanker always had many electric primers at hand…

The 8.8cm KwK 36 allowed artillery type mission to be carried out but with certain limitations. The sPzAbt 503 reported after a successful combat firing using the *Höhen-Richtaufsatz* (sight mount) that the sight was to be used for ranges beyond 4,000m. Under this distance the standard telescopic gun sight was easier to handle. The unit noted that the slow velocity SprGrPatr

(HE round) took more than 18 seconds to travel to a target at a distance of 8km. Both crosswind and the rifling in the gun barrel could impair the trajectory of the projectile, these factors had to be considered during aiming. To be sure of hitting a target, gunners had to use bracketing.

The unit reported from a *Gefechtsschiessen* (combat firing) of 12 June 1943:

Target	Range	Ammunition
T-34	1,800m	Two PzGr
Gun position, 4.5cm AT gun	1,400m	Six SprGr
Gun position, 7.62cm AT gun	4,800m	Five SprGr

Secondary armament

One *Maschinengewehr* 34 (MG 34) for close defense was mounted in the right-hand side of the hull in front of the radio operator. A further MG 34 was mounted coaxially in the main gun mantlet.

Further means of defence

The Tiger was fitted with a smoke grenade discharger mounted on each side of the turret. This device was used in case of an emergency withdrawal under a cloud of dense smoke. During the first heavy engagements, however, these devices proved to be easily ignited by enemy small arms fire or shell splinters, causing visibility problems for the tank crew. For this reason the turret-mounted smoke dischargers were removed. By 1944, a new device the *Nahverteidigungswaffe* (close-defense weapon) was introduced. This was a grenade launcher fired from the inside the tank using either smoke or

A Tiger Ausf E of III/PzRgt "Grossdeutschland" moves past other tanks from the regiment. The Tiger's front was packed with extra track links. Although officially forbidden, the crew apparently felt better. The Befehlspanther in the background seems to carry the marking, "0", denoting it as the vehicle of Oberst Willi Langkeit. (Schneider)

Cleaning the gun barrel was an arduous task. Four men were required to push and pull the Rohrwischer (a large stiff brush) through the bore in order to remove any metal or powder residues from the rifling. (Anderson)

splinter-type shells. The smoke shell was used to lay a screen over the tank, the splinter shell was fired to detonate above the tank to wound or kill any enemy (and sometimes own) infantry in close proximity to the tank.

Combat reports

Hauptmann Lange, commander of 2/sPzAbt 502 in his report dated 29 January 1943:

> ...Fire fight:
> The most favorable distance is 1,500m with well adjusted weapons we got clear hits only. Impact and penetration is so far without any complaint. The ratio between HE and AP rounds must be 1:1...

From an after action report of sPzAbt 503 dated 15 March 1943:

> The following experiences of the *Abteilung* are available:
> 1.) 7.5cm (Kurz) *Granatpatrone* 38 Hl (as used with the PzKfw III Ausf N)
> 2.) 8.8cm *Panzergranate*
>
> 1.) Success against enemy tanks at minimal ammunition consumption was possible only at ranges under 1,000m...
>
> 2.) Success against enemy tanks was possible at any ranges, the most favourable range was between 1,200 and 2,000m. At 2,000m the first round will be a hit, a second round was only occasionally necessary. It is possible to engage enemy tanks in clear visibility at more distant ranges. One PzKpfw VI destroyed five T-34 (three crossing in front) at ranges between 2,500 and 3,000m. Only 18 rounds were fired...

An after action report of 13.Kp (Tiger-Kp) of PzRgt *"Grossdeutschland"* dated 27 March 1943 reveals:

The 8.8cm KwK proved to be a reliable and effective weapon. No faults or damage to the electric firing mechanism or similar occurred. No more than three rounds were necessary to achieve direct hits on marching artillery columns at 5,000m range using HE shells. Horses and men lay in the snow immediately. At ranges of 1,500m and more we achieved many hits on T-34 using the *Panzer-Kopfgranate* (AP round) with low ammunition consumption...

...General and technical experiences:

During a scouting missions two Tigers encountered some 20 Russian tanks frontally. Further enemy tanks attacked from the rear. An encounter developed, in which tank and weapon performed outstandingly. Both Tigers received ten or more hits at ranges between 600 and 1,000m, for the most part from 7.62 cm guns. The armour protection withstood from all angles. No penetration was achieved. Even hits in the running gear, which tore away torsion bars, did not cause a breakdown. While the hits struck the armour, the commander, gunner and loader could designate, aim and fire at targets unchallenged. Weak smoke emissions and flakes of interior paint could be extracted by the turret ventilator.

Result: Kill of ten enemy tanks by two Tigers within 15 minutes.

Most times the first shot was a hit at ranges between 600 to 1,000m. At these ranges the *Panzergranate* produced an absolute destructive penetration to the frontal armour, and demolished the engine in the rear, too. In only a few cases the T-34 was torched. Hits at the same ranges to the sides or rear led to an explosion of the fuel in 80 per cent of all cases. Even at ranges of 1,500m and more, with favourable weather conditions, similar results were achieved with low ammunition usage. Experiences with HE shells could not be made due to the severe shortage of this ammunition.

The Paderborn training courses (*Tiger-Lehrgang*) noted proudly in a report dated 29 May 1943:

....The KwK 8.8cm shows extraordinary good impact and penetration. The most favourable firing ranges are around 2,000m. In one case in Russia, a Tiger with good observation and raised slope position managed to destroy five T-34 (three in parallel movement) and a 7.62cm AT gun at ranges between 2,200 and 3,000m using only 18 AP and HE shells. In North Africa, the General Sherman (M4) was destroyed at the following ranges: 3,400m frontal penetration in the gearbox; at 600m punched penetration and torn out exit at the rear. All other emerging enemy tanks were penetrated as well. The crews are fully satisfied with this gun...

Pages 82/83
Crew of a Tiger from sPzAbt 501 rush to examine damage to the running gear. A long halt on an open road without any cover could prove to be very dangerous. This is a late production Ausf E Befehlstiger (command tank), note the radio antenna visible behind the open hatch. The winter camouflage has been hand-applied in the field by the crew. The combat tracks are fitted with ice cleats. (Kadari)

The Tiger Ausf E had stowage for 92 rounds of ammunition in the fighting compartment. Some crews used every free space to increase this amount. This Tiger Ausf E from sPzAbt 502 is fitted with the original compliment of 12 smoke grenade dischargers, six on the turret and six on the hull. These were soon removed by units in the field as they could easily be ignited by infantry fire or shrapnel. The dischargers were not fitted to later versions. (Münch)

Optics

sPzAbt 503 in a report dated 15 March 1943:

…The optical equipment on the Pzkpfw VI fully meets the troops´ demands. We suggest the following improvements:

1.) The exterior glasses of the double telescope often show condensation and accumulation of dirt. We demand a wiper for the optics, leather is better than felt.

2.) The rigid graduated range plate in the left tube of the double telescope should be moveable as is the right tube, so both tubes of the stereoscopic telescope can be used separately when one is damaged…

3.) The gunner needs a telescope [in the turret roof] near the turret lamp, as on the T-34.

The Tiger Ausf B

Even before the Tiger Ausf E was issued to the first units, work on a successor had started. The PzKpfw VI Tiger Ausf B should exceed it in every aspect. An important part of this development was an improved gun with higher muzzle velocity, resulting in even better armour penetration.

By 1941, Rheinmetall presented the 8.8cm FlaK 41 as a successor to the 8.8cm FlaK 36/37. Hitler was apparently impressed by the long barrel (L/74) and the ballistic data. Subsequently, he (and his cohorts) demanded the development of a tank gun based on this weapon. By 1 July 1942, the *Überblick über den Stand der Entwicklungen beim Heer* (survey on developments of the army) noted:

8.8cm KwK 41
Demand: Successor for the 8.8 cm KwK 36 for VK 45.01 (Porsche)…

Since late 1941, the *schwere Panzerabwehrkanone* (sPaK) programme was launched with the objective to expedite the introduction of powerful tank guns capable of destroying Soviet heavy tanks. By late 1942, this culminated in the 8.8cm PaK 43/41 which had been developed from the FlaK 41. The PaK 43/41 had an impressive ballistic performance and was being issued to combat forces by April 1943.

After six-month development the new tank gun was ready for production. The first 50 PzKpfw VI Tiger Ausf B built were mounted with the 8.8cm KwK 43 L/72, fitted with a one-piece barrel. On all further Tiger Ausf B to be built and fitted with the later series turret, the KwK 43 had a two-piece barrel, which was easier to manufacture.

The Tiger-Fibel contained pages with data on where to hit an enemy tank. These included the so-called Kleeblätter (Shamrocks). The green sector defined a combat situation where the respective enemy tank could damage or destroy the Tiger. The larger red sector clearly shows the superiority of the Tiger tank where it could destroy the enemy tank, but remain immune to return fire. (Anderson)

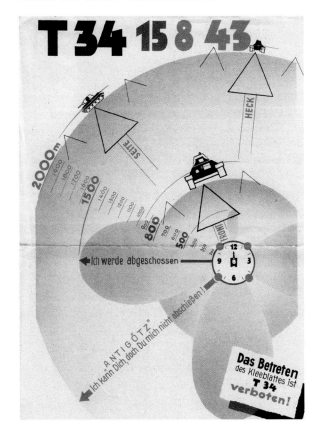

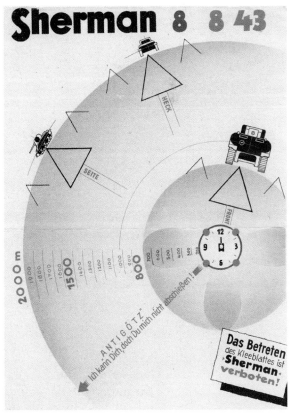

Unlike the 8.8cm KwK 36, it is difficult to find accurate information on the KwK 43. Military archives only contain a few data sheets. On the other hand, the internet offers a lot of technical detail, much of which cannot be verified.

A document published by the OKH (supreme command of the army) dated April 1943 gives some information on armour penetration of the 8.8cm PaK 43 L/71 and KwK 43. The PzGrPatr 39-1 is listed and the PzGrPatr 40/43 is mentioned to be in planning stage. Penetration data on both rounds are given (see below). An HL (hollow charge – HEAT) round is not mentioned in this list. However, the *Datenblatt* G 24I detailed a similar round.

The 8.8cm SprGrPatr 43, KwK 43 was an HE round, which could be fired with or without a delay fuse.

The 8.8cm PzGrPatr 39/43, KwK 43 was the standard AP ammunition.

The 8.8cm PzGrPatr 40/43, KwK 43 was a *Hartkern* (tungsten core) armour-piercing shot, again with outstanding performance.

The 8.8cm GrPatr 39 (HL), KwK 43 was a hollow-charge round for use against tanks.

The following penetration data can be found in German wartime documents:

Range:	100m	500m	1,000m	1,500m	2,000m
8.8cm PzGrPatr 39/43	202	185	165	148	132
8.8cm PzGrPatr 40/43	237	217	193	170	152

All after action reports dealing with the weapon (mostly the 8.8cm PaK 43/41 or PaK 43) do not mention the exact type of projectile fired, they only refer to a *Panzergranate*. The existence of the most efficient *Hartkern* round (PzGrPatr 40/43) in greater numbers is doubtful.

Combat experiences

The high-performance gun required a lot of space inside the turret for the recoil after firing.

Karl Fischer, a veteran of sPzAbt 503 recalls:

> ...I was loader in a *Königstiger* [Tiger B]. At the age of 19, I was physically fit and strong. The handling of the large shots [length approximately 1m, weight 20kg] inside the turret, which was not that spacious, was difficult. I never got that many bruises in all my life...

In the archives, there are not many after action reports from PzKpfw VI Tiger B units which have survived. However, the weapon was used by anti-tank units equipped with the 8.8cm PaK 43/41 (towed anti-tank gun) or the SdKfz 164 *Hornisse* (Hornet) self-propelled gun. Both used the same ordnance as the Tiger Ausf B.

A Tiger Ausf E of sPzAbt 501 in North Africa during the spring of 1943. The fighting here showed the absolute superiority of the Tiger over any Allied tank. The last months of tank battles in Tunisia demonstrated the effectiveness of tactics first deployed by German forces between 1940 and 1942. (NARA)

The "shamrock" for the British Churchill tank, which German tank crews classified as a difficult tank to fight. Great numbers were encountered in Russia, which had been supplied under the Lend-Lease programme. According to some sources 40 per cent of the types used by the Soviet Army on the southern front were either US or British-built tanks. (Anderson)

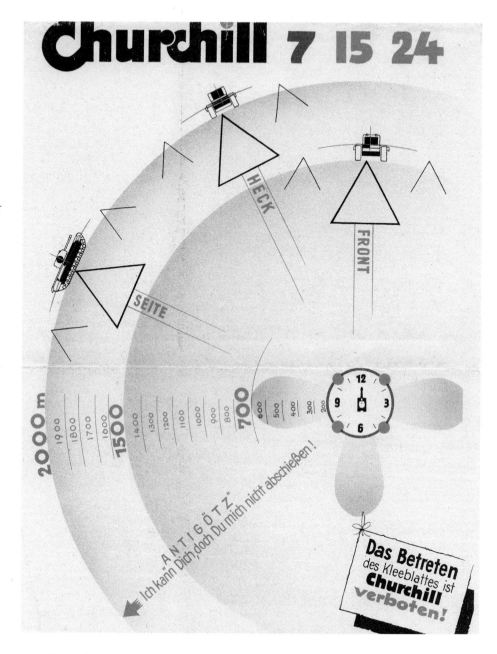

The *schwere Heeres-Panzerjäger-Abteilung* 662 (sHPzJgAbt 662) was equipped with 8.8cm PaK 43/41 L/71 which had identical performance data to the KwK 43. In an after action report dated 1 August 1943 that commander notes:

> … the accuracy of the gun was extraordinarily good, in some cases enemy tanks were shot up at ranges up to 5,000m… Frequent readjustment of the gun is required…

The sPzJgAbt 655 reported on 27 August 1943:

> ...the company, (six *Hornisse*) was from 11 July until 27 July deployed in the defense battles east of Orel... We destroyed: one KV-2, 19 KV-1, one General Lee (M3), 30 T-34, one T-60 and five T-70 tanks...

Technical experiences:
The 8.8cm PaK 43/41 has proved its value. Fire could be opened at wide ranges. The impact was destructive with all enemy tanks. In one incident we destroyed a T-34 at a distance of 4,200m...

The sPzJgAbt 519, equipped with *Hornisse*, in a combat report dated 28 February 1944:

> ...During the defense of Vitebsk the Russians launched mass attacks with 50 or more tanks... Within 27 minutes 22 out of 47 attacking tanks were destroyed at no own loss. One *Hornisse* destroyed 14, another destroyed six, and a third two tanks...

A PzKpfw VI Tiger Ausf E from sPzAbt 508 captured intact by troops from 22nd Battalion, 4th Brigade, 2nd New Zealand Division at Romola (north of Florence, Italy) on 2 August, 1944. (IWM)

The PzKpfw VI Tiger followed the proven German principles of tank design. Although often misunderstood as a direct answer to the Soviet T-34 tank, the Tiger was an evolutionary development.

The head of the development team, Dr. Erwin Aders, can be quoted (from Spielberger, *The PzKpfw Tiger and its variants*):

> ...Even by September or October 1942, the PzKpfw Tiger Ausf E was called a lame duck by the authorities. The turret, which had been designed by Krupp, was cylindrical and after deliberation the shape was compared to a tin can...

By 1942 standards, armour protection on the PzKpfw VI Tiger was indeed impressive. The front parts of both the hull and turret were 100mm thick, while the sides and rear plates had a thickness of 80mm. The fact that the main surfaces of the hull were practically vertical did not affect the high standard of armour protection for the crew. By the end of 1942, the Allies did not have a gun or the ammunition to cause any damage to a PzKpfw VI Tiger at any range over 100m. However, on the Eastern Front the Russians fought with any gun available – the Tiger was exposed to fire from many different types including the 14.5mm anti-tank rifle up to the 15.2cm howitzer.

1943 – The year of the Tiger

When the PzKpfw VI entered service it appeared to fulfill the dreams of any tank crew. Virtually indestructible and mounting the astonishingly deadly 8.8cm cannon – a scenario which the Nazi propaganda machine found irresistible.

An after action report of 13.Kp (Tiger-Kp) of PzRgt "Grossdeutschland" dated 27 March 1943 provides an impression of the reality of tank warfare. Also the undeniable qualities of the armour on the Tiger.

A Tiger Ausf E of sPzAbt 502 has received a direct hit from a Soviet 7.62cm tank gun. The round bounced-off leaving only a small indentation without harming the tank crew. (Münch)

The tank "231" of Leutnant Zabel from sPzAbt 503 was hit 252 times by fire from all calibres during combat near Ssemernikovo. The tank was able to be driven a further 60km and returned to the unit. Later, the tank was returned to Germany (note the transport tracks) but it is not known whether this tank was repaired. (Anderson)

Leutnant Zabel... reported this attack near Ssemernikovo kolkhoz:

The combat group Sander had to face a very strong enemy when attacking the collective farm west of Ssemernikovo. The Tiger attacking as advance platoon left the lighter tanks behind, and attracted all the enemy fire. The tanks received hits on the front and to the right-hand side. The enemy, with tanks, AT guns and AT rifles opened fire at a great distance. My Tiger received a 7.62cm hit in the front of the driver's position. The spare track links fixed there with an iron rod were ripped off. In the tank we noticed a bang and a slight shaking. The nearer we came, the stronger the bangs and shaking from the 7.62cm hits became. At the same time we noticed considerably high dust clouds from artillery ground impacts near the tank. Further on, the crew noticed a somewhat lighter bang followed by a burst of yellow smoke, most likely a hit from an AT rifle.

A short time later we received a hit from a 4.5cm AT gun on the cupola. The brackets of the bullet-proof glass were smashed. The glass vision block jammed and became opaque caused by heat from the explosion. A further hit destroyed the brackets and the hatch fell into the turret interior. There was dense smoke in the fighting compartment and the area became very hot. The loader's hatch was jammed and stood slightly open and it received a number of hits from AT rifles demolishing the hinges and brackets.

After the battle two 4.5cm AT guns and 15 AT rifle hits were counted on the cupola.

On both days of the attack the enemy destroyed our machine guns. The smoke dischargers on the turret were also destroyed. The smoke in the turret caused so much trouble that the Tiger was not ready for action for some time...

...all crew members nerves were frayed, we lost our sense of time. We felt neither hunger nor any other needs. Despite the fact that the attack lasted for more than six hours, all men in the tank felt the time had gone by in a flash.

After a further 7.62cm hit on the mantlet the gun mounting bolts sheared off. The recoil brake lost its fluid and the gun barrel remained in rear (recoiled) position. Due to electric problems the breech block could not be shut. Due to shocks inflicted by further hits the radio system failed and the steering levers were jammed. When the exhaust cover was destroyed, the engine caught fire. This fire could be extinguished by the fire-fighting system. Further hits loosened some turret ring screws. The turret traversing system failed temporarily...

We counted 227 hits by AT rifles, 14 hits by 5.7cm AT guns and 11 hits by 7.62cm AT guns. The right suspension was heavily damaged by shelling. The connecting pieces for several running wheels were ruined, two torsion bars were broken. A rear idler wheel bearing was damaged.

In spite of this damage the Tiger was able to be driven for further 60km. The hits inflicted cracks to some weld seams. A fuel tank began leaking due to the

After the combat, "231" was loaded on an SSyms railway wagon for transport back to Germany. Note the air filters on the rear of the hull have been blown off. The gun mantlet has received many hits from Soviet anti-tank (AT) rifles in an attempt to damage the sighting telescope. Also the cupola has received many well-aimed, but ineffective hits. (Anderson)

D 656/27

Tiger

... Mapß, jooo un Tiglittu ! –

The first page of the Tiger-Fibel, the text reads: "The Tiger… Blimey! What a hot rod". (Anderson)

heavy shocks. We noticed a number of impacts in the track links, which however did not particularly impair mobility.

Subsequently, it can be said that the armour on the Tiger had come up to our expectations...

Signed Lt. Zabel

The discovery that Soviet AT weapons were of reasonable quality and effectiveness was quite a shock for the German invaders of 1941. The majority of German *Panzerjäger* units were still equipped with the 3.7cm PaK anti-tank gun, which became obsolete almost over night (following battle experience during the *Blitzkrieg* on France). The Soviet Army had the 7.62cm field gun, which soon became known as a weapon powerful enough able to destroy every type of German tank. This gun was known to the *Landser* (German trooper) as the *Ratsch-Bumm* a weapon with a high muzzle velocity – *Ratsch* the sound of the impact would be heard earlier than the bang (*Bumm*) when the gun was fired. Along with many different types of AT guns the Soviet Army had the 14.5mm AT rifle. Even today this gun is unjustly reported to have been "obsolete" and "ineffective", but this

Er fällt alles aus....

Dieser Tiger erhielt im Südabschnitt in 6 Stunden:

> 227 Treffer Panzerbüchse,
> 14 Treffer 5,2 cm und
> 11 Treffer 7,62 cm.

Keiner ging durch.

Laufrollen und Verbindungsstücke waren zerschossen,

2 Schwingarme arbeiteten nicht mehr,

mehrere Pak-Treffer saßen genau auf der Kette, und

auf 3 Minen war er gefahren.

Er fuhr mit eigener Kraft noch 60 km Gelände.

man portable weapon had a number of advantages being easy to produce and inexpensive, allowing it to be issued in vast numbers. In the hands of brave soldiers willing to risk their lives, the AT rifle could penetrate the side armour of most German light armoured vehicles including the *Sturmgeschütze*. The command cupola, mounted on the top of the turret, was especially liable to damage by the explosive impact this weapon.

Even a PzKpfw VI could be seriously damaged by an AT rifle. A chance hit on a glass vision block in the cupola could injure the commander whereas a hit on the driver's vision visor could halt a Tiger tank.

The Paderborn training course noted their experience in a report dated 19 May 1943:

> …With the exception of the American 5.7cm AT gun the Tiger proved to be safe against frontal and lateral fire from any AT weapon, including captured German 7.5 cm PaK. The penetrations by 5.7cm AT gun resulted from hits to the sides of the hull and turret. As a result from hits inflicted by a 7.62cm gun, some significant damage occurred: jamming of the main gun and MG mantlet, shearing screws and bolts, breakdown of radio and electrical systems. This damage led to temporary loss of the Tiger. After fire from a 7.62cm gun

Quite naturally, the extraordinary story of "231" was picked up and used by the Nazi propaganda machine. Furthermore, a photograph of the tank was used in the Tiger-Fibel published in early 1943. Note the damaged smoke grenade discharger. (Anderson)

at close range, cracks in the front plate and the gun mantlet occurred. The Russian anti-tank rifle, which is able to put the Panzer III and IV out of action, is no threat to the Tiger. It managed to punch 4cm holes at very close range. AT rifle fire to the glass vision blocks will destroy the visor. Direct hits will penetrate the glass block therefore the visor slit must be kept as narrow as possible. Even 7.62cm hits to the drive sprocket did not always lead to a breakdown of the Tiger…

The "American 5.7cm AT gun" was possibly the British Ordnance 6 pounder QF, which was adopted by the US Army as the 57mm Gun M1. However, the introduction of any new threat on the battlefield, such as the Tiger tank, would have unavoidably led to counter measures being produced. The Soviets did their best to deal with the superior Tiger by developing and producing longer-barrelled (larger calibre) guns and improved armour piercing ammunition.

Apparently, many German military leaders had illusions regarding the potential of the Tiger tank. Through hasty and tactically wrong deployment of this powerful (and vital) battlefield asset many were lost. All this was avoidable. A *Panzeroffizier* warned military leaders in a letter dated 12 September 1943:

Soviet anti-tank (AT) guns could stop a PzKpfw VI Tiger. Here one hit has penetrated the turret just above the numeral 2, and another one next to the tactical number. A third has penetrated and lifted the cupola. (Anderson)

Far Left
A Kradmelder (dispatch rider) in the freezing conditions of a Russian winter. A Tiger Ausf E from sPzAbt 501 has been thoroughly camouflaged leaving only the tactical number visible. (Anderson)

A Tiger Ausf E of sPzAbt 505 (note the "Charging Bull" unit badge) captured in Russia. After the battle it appears to have been used to train Soviet gunners. The tank has received a large number of hits, including clean penetrations. (Netrebenko)

Many military authorities, especially those at higher levels, seem to believe that the Tiger is invulnerable. I herewith state:

The *Panzerkampfwagen* VI Tiger is not impregnable, in fact the tank can be penetrated by the Russian 7.62cm gun (long barrel) at favourable angle of impact:

Frontally at ranges up to	500m
Sides and rear up to ranges of	1,500m

... According to Soviet Army notes the Tiger can be penetrated by:

Gun	Ammunition	Front	Side	Rear
45mm M 37	Subcalibre	--	200m	200m
45mm M 42	Subcalibre	--	500m	500m
57mm	Subcalibre	500m		
	AP shot	--	600m	600m
76mm AA	Subcalibre	700m		
	AP shot	--	500m	500m
76mm AT	Subcalibre	100m	700m	700m
85mm AA	AP shot	--	1,000m	1,000m
122mm	AP shot	1,000m	1,500m	1,500m
152mm	AP shot	500m	1,000m	1,000m

In just a year after the Tiger entered service the invulnerability of the tank had to be put into perspective. Very much as in 1942, all attacks had to be thoroughly planned and prepared as any action could result in losses, even to the mighty Tiger. Bearing in mind the relative low number of operational Tigers during any offensive action a certain amount of risk would be existent.

Tiger Ausf B

As the successor to the Ausf E, it was logical to expect that the Tiger Ausf B would have an enhanced level of armour protection. Along with the increase in the thickness of the armour, the general layout of the tank was dramatically changed. Very much like the PzKpfw V Panther medium tank, the hull of the Tiger Ausf B was built with sloping armour.

In comparison to the Tiger Ausf E the frontal armour was significantly increased. The front of the hull had a thickness of 150mm, the turret front 185mm and all other side plates were 80mm thick.

However, this improvement in defensive armour brought about a significant increase in weight, and subsequently limited mobility. At 72 tons, a damaged or broken down tank could not just be hauled away by the overstretched recovery troops.

From the beginning of Operation *Citadel* many crews from sPzAbt 505, tied barbed wire to the hull of the Tiger in an effort to deter Soviet close combat teams from climbing on the tank. Apparently this method was retained during the following winter. (Anderson)

Two clean hits have penetrated the 100mm armour of the front plate of this Tiger Ausf E. (Anderson)

The hull of a PzKpfw VI Tiger Ausf B used after the war for test firings by the US military. The 150mm armour has not been penetrated by HVAP shots from 90 and 105mm guns, which at that time were the most powerful US-manufactured anti-tank weapons in service. (NARA)

The *Nachrichtblatt der Panzertruppen* dated Feburary 1945 noted:

...Tank versus Tank combat in the West.

The effective combat ranges of own and hostile tanks are dependent on the fire positions and in particular from the position of the tanks to each other. That is to say whether combat is front to front or against the flanks. Based on experiences made at the front and by shooting trials the following can be stated:

...Thanks to its penetration the Tiger is far superior to the Sherman, with the exception of the gun mantlet it will be punched at all places at ranges up to 3,000m, while the Sherman cannot penetrate the Tiger´s front at all, and the sides at ranges from 1,100 to 1,800m.

The report does not define the version of Tiger and neither does it indentify the type gun in the Sherman. Surely it made a difference as to whether a 75mm or a 76mm gun was engaged.

The German authorities did not ignore the fact that the Tiger could be vulnerable. The company commanders, platoon leaders, and the crews were urged to adapt their tactical deployment to the changed conditions. Again from the *Nachrichtenblatt der Panzertruppe*, Volume 4, September 1944:

...Single Tigers may not take positions on heights to observe the terrain! At such an occasion three Tigers were shot up recently by direct 122mm hits, killing all but two crewmen...

A Tiger from sPzAbt 508 destroyed by US forces in Italy, 1944. The impact of the armour-piercing (AP) round has chipped off large areas of the Zimmerit anti-magnetic coating. (US Signal Corps)

Combat 6

Combat on the Eastern Front: 1942 and 1943

Alfred Rubbel, a veteran of sPzAbt 503 recalls:

> I met my first Tiger at Putlos. I was there for occupational retraining. Alas, there was no Tiger at hand by January 1943... We killed the time with the movies – and with the landlord's daughters... By the end of January my friend Heino rushed into the canteen: "It's here! The first Tiger is here..." We ran to the vehicle halls. It was quite a shock for me. I do not know what I indeed had expected. We had fought the T-34 at the *Ostfront*, we waited for a tank with sleek, elegant lines. How great was the disappointment to see this massive block of iron...

The establishment of the first unit, sPzAbt 502 proceeded at a rather slow pace. By August 1942, nine Tigers were issued to the *Abteilung* and ordered to the *Heeresgruppe Nord* near the town of Mga. No command tanks were available at that time.

An unkown officer complains the inappropriate way the Tigers were sent into their first combat:

> ...the situation of PzAbt 301 and sPzAbt 502 will be close to the honoured general's heart. I must state that it cannot go on like that anymore. According to the after action reports present to me three of the new Tigers were shot up almost immediately, because they were irresponsibly employed in mined terrain against several dug-in T-34...

The standard German procedures for preparing an attack were recklessly ignored. The reconnaissance results were not properly analyzed, and if this

Generalfeldmarschall Rommel inspects one of the first Tiger Ausf E, possibly in Kummersdorf. The front track guards are a temporary fitting and the heavy towing shackles are not the standard type. By September 1942 the first two Tigers had been delivered to Rommel. (Kadari)

The crew of this Tiger, possibly from sPzAbt 502, is refuelling the tank from "Jerrycans" during operations in Russia, 1943. The turret has received many hits from Soviet anti-tank (AT) rifles and guns. (Anderson)

were so, the wrong conclusions were drawn. Possibly the higher command ordered this attack disregarding the unit commander. With a new, unproven tank any such action will turn out to be risky as the crews were not familiar with the vehicle and operational data was not available. In this situation, the first deployment must be called a failure.

By April 1943, AOK 18 published a report on the fighting from 12 January until 31 March 1943:

A. *Panzer*

Deployment of 1/sPzAbt 502 was effected in three phases:

1.) 12 January – 5 February	south of Ladoga lake near Ssinjavino
2.) 12 – 17 February	near Michkino, Tchernychevo and Porkusy
3.) 19 – 31 March	south of Krassnij Bor (mission not accomplished)

	1.)	2.)	3.)
Maximum number of deployed tanks per day (inc. newly issued tanks)	Six PzKpfw VI 15 PzKpfw III	Three PzKpfw VI Three PzKpfw III	Four PzKpfw VI Three PzKpfw III

Rate of tanks destroyed	55	57	48
Own losses	43 men	Six men	Three men
	Six PzKpfw VI	Three PzKpfw VI	--
	12 PzKpfw III	One PzKpfw III	--

Notes:

Re. 1)
On 12 January 1943, the company combined with a PzGrenRgt for a counter-attack. A succession of deployments followed for local counter-attacks, covering missions in platoon strength and single-actions over difficult terrain.

Re. 2)
One mission was to attack an enemy assembly position (destroying 31 tanks)

A Tiger Ausf E from sPzAbt 502, one of the batch delivered by summer 1942. The tank retains the small front track guards but lacks those on the side of the hull. (Münch)

Panzergrenadiere (armoured infantry) advance under the cover of a Tiger Ausf E from sPzAbt 502. Being too close to the Tiger could be dangerous, as any enemy gun would open fire at the tank. But infantry had to be available to attack Soviet anti-tank teams. (Anderson)

Re. 3)

Mainly a deployment with the order to destroy enemy tanks advancing along the track. Missions to support own infantry fighting in woods could not be accomplished due to soft ground and damage to own weapons. Surprise attacks against enemy positions after exhaustive reconnaissance with good results.

B. *Sturmgeschütze*

1.) Deployment of StuGAbt 226 over the period

　　a) Number of StuG deployed including replacements:　　41

　　b) Number of enemy tanks destroyed:　　210

　　c) Losses of own personnel:　　95

Material (total losses):　　13

2.) Deployment of StuGBttr of 1, 10, 12 and 13 LwFeldDiv
    a) Number of StuG deployed including replacements: 20
    b) Number of enemy tank destroyed: 17
    c) Losses of own personnel: 34
Material (total losses):   5

3.) Notes:
StuGAbt 226 was deployed in battery and platoon strength, the *Sturmgeschütze* of the *Luftwaffe* were deployed to observe the *Sturmgeschütz-Abteilung* in order to give them the opportunity to achieve missing combat experience, and because their lack of technical training and equipment made this necessary.

C. *Panzerjäger*
The number of anti-tank guns ready-for-action deployed by the army was to average:

253 *mittlere* (medium) mPaK
383 *schwere* (heavy) sPaK (towed and self-propelled)

The deployment of mPak and sPaK suffered from limited mobility. Even for the sPaK newly issued by 10 February 1943, no prime movers with cross-country mobility were available. Thus establishment of points of main effort in the *Korps* was not possible. The number of available sPak was never sufficient anyway.

    Points of main effort could only be established by the Army equipped with prime movers and utilization of withdrawn and battle-weary divisions. Depending on the combat situation a maximum 50 sPaK were thus available.

D. Overview:
In the period 12 January to 31 March 1943
        697 enemy tanks were destroyed
        172 enemy tanks were immobilized
  In total   869

This number breaks down as follows:
a) StuGAbt 226   210
    StuG of LwFeld-Div   17   227
b) Tanks (1/sPzAbt 502)   160
                        387

d) 47 tanks were destroyed by 8.8cm FlaK
e) 435 tanks were destroyed by sPaK

This interesting report on the battles around Lake Ladoga near Leningrad reveals a lot of information. The numbers given allow an evaluation of own tank kills and losses. The sPzAbt 502 had reached an impressive score, especially during mission No.3 dated 19 March to 31 March 1943. Four PzKpfw VI, assisted by three PzKpfw III destroyed 48 enemy tanks

Pages 108/109
Tigers from sPzAbt 502 parked and ready for maintenance by the workshop company. The tank (possibly from the staff company) appears to have an engine problem and a large canvas awning has been erected over the rear of the vehicle to allow engineers to work in the dry. (Münch)

without losses. The two earlier missions were also a success, but with a loss of 24 tanks. Summarized, the missions gave a kill ratio of approximately 7 to 1. However, the Tiger did not fight alone; StuGAbt 226 equipped with the feared *Sturmgeschütze* (StuG) was also most successful. With 41 assault guns 210 enemy tanks were destroyed, against 13 StuG lost. A ratio of 16 to 1, a most impressive score. Apparently it was possible to defeat great numbers of Soviet tanks with relatively standard equipment.

The *Luftwaffe-Felddivisonen* (Air Force Field Division) fighting with the army did not function to a similar degree. Equipped with *Sturmgeschütze* instead of towed AT guns as *Panzerjäger-Kompanien* (tank hunter company), the crews were not sufficiently trained in *Sturmgeschütz* tactics and the small number of assault guns available never did allow for a concentrated deployment. For this reason the *Luftwaffe Sturmgeschütze* were under the command of *Sturmgeschütz Abteilung* 226, and followed their advance closely in order to learn. If the statistics are true, their score ratio was approximately 3 to 1. This example shows severe shortcomings in equipping the *Luftwaffe-Feldivisions*, and all other infantry units being issued with *Sturmgeschütze* after autumn 1942. The StuG was not a *Panzerjäger* (tank destroyer).

The performance of the towed or *Selbstfahrlafette* (self-propelled [SP]) anti-tank guns is most interesting. Far more than 50 per cent of the 869 tanks destroyed or immobilized in the period were destroyed by anti-tank (AT) guns. Unfortunately, as there is no detailed information available noting the exact numbers of the SP guns, a comparable ratio cannot be determined.

The sPzAbt 502, employed at the Army Group North, had to release the 2nd Company to reinforce other the units near Stalingrad. The remaining two companies fought around Leningrad, some 1,500km north and 2/sPzAbt 502 was subordinated under sPzAbt 503 to become 3/sPzAbt 503. By 14 April 1943, the unit was still short of equipment, with only a few operational Tigers. A total of four Tiger, one PzKpfw III (lang) and two PzKpfw III (Kurz) were reported ready for action (e). Two Tigers and one PzKpfw III (lang) were in need for repair (i). None were to be delivered (z).

14 April 1943 (e) Four PzKpfw VI, one PzKpfw III (lang), two PzKpfw III (Kurz)
(i) Two PzKpfw VI,one PzKpfw III (lang)

22 April 1943 (e) Five PzKpfw VI, one PzKpfw III (lang), one PzLpfw III (Kurz)
(i) One PzKpfw VI, two PzKpfw III (lang)

04 May 1943 (e) Five PzKpfw VI, one PzKpfw III (lang), one PzKpfw III (Kurz)
(i) One PzKpfw VI, two PzKpfw III (lang)

11 May 1943 (e) Five PzKpfw VI, one PzKpfw III (lang),
one PzKpfw III (Kurz)
(i) Two PzKpfw VI, two PzKpfw III (lang)

21 May 1943 (e) Five PzKpfw VI, one PzKpfw III (lang),
one PzKpfw III (Kurz)
(i) Two PzKpfw VI, two PzKpfw III (lang)

02 June 1943 (e) Six PzKpfw VI, one PzKpfw III (lang),
two PzKpfw III (Kurz)
(i) One PzKpfw VI, one PzKpfw III (lang)
(z) Seven PzKpfw VI

The constant supply of ammunition and fuel was vital for Tiger units operating on the battlefield. Tank "312" is replenished with 8.8cm rounds after action in the early spring of 1943. Note the number has been stenciled on the side of the turret and also on the side of the hull. (Münch)

Infantrymen travel on a Tiger Ausf E from an unknown unit. Due to the lack of railway routes in the East many Tigers had to be driven over long distances under their own power. The additional maintenance required had an effect on operational readiness. (Anderson)

10 June 1943	(e) Six PzKpfw VI, one PzKpfw III (lang), two PzKpfw III (Kurz)
	(i) One PzKpfw VI, one PzKpfw III (lang)
	(z) Seven PzKpfw VI
01 July 1943	(e) Eleven PzKpfw VI, one PzKpfw III (lang), two PzKpfw III (Kurz)
	(i) Three PzKpfw VI, one PzKpfw III (lang)
	(z) Thirty-three PzKpfw VI (including two Beflswg)
12 July 1943	(e) Eleven PzKpfw VI, one PzKpfw III (lang) three PzKpfw III (Kurz)
	(i) Three PzKpfw VI
	(z) Thirty-one PzKpfw VI (including two Bflswg.)

07 July 1943   (e) Forty-five PzKpfw VI

10 August 1943   (e) Thirteen PzKpfw VI
                 (i) Seventeen PzKpfw VI (Kurz), 12 (lang)

7 July 1943   Total losses Three PzKpfw VI Tiger

The higher army levels waited for after action reports. *Hauptmann* Lange, commander of 2/sPzAbt 502 wrote a statement relating to his first battles at *Heeresgruppe* Don (Army Group Don) on 29 January 1943:

Analysis:
It must be made clear by strict orders at headquarters at all levels not to use Tiger-units below company strength. Panzer IV and Panzer III must never be separated. The Tiger must be a battering ram in the proceeding advance and buffer at the focal point of the defense… There is always the risk that Tiger units get orders, which can be solved by normal tank units without problems. Due to steady relocation engine and suspension will be heavily strained, the lack of time impedes necessary maintenance and repair works. Thus Tiger units fall out when they are not needed.

Enemy fire:
Fire by 7.62cm AT gun gave no penetration or heavy damage to all Tigers of the company. In one case, a direct hit at the upper frontal edge of the cupola shifted it slightly cracking the welded seam. The Russian AT rifle attained bullet holes of up to 17mm depth…

Fire fight:
The most favourable firing distance was up to 100m. Carefully adjusted weapons gained clear hits. Impact and penetration of the 8.8cm at all targets was efficient…

Proposals of amendments:
Commander: The cupola must be designed to be less prominent. The turret hatch has to swivel laterally…
Loader: The MG is situated too close to the gun…
Driver: Visor blocks easily damaged
Wireless operator: Position is very cramped. Command tanks need MW radio set to reach the division.

Organization:
The sPzAbt with two companies has a great potential fighting power. An increase by a 3rd (Tiger) company, as it is occasionally strived for, is inappropriate. Such massing of Tigers is not possible at the moment. The *Abteilung* will be separated, with great problems for the supply services. Furthermore the *Abteilung* will become less mobile, becoming unable to fulfill its tasks…

Tiger combat in North Africa

In response to the British success in their offensive at El Alamein, on 2 November 1942 the OKH Operations *Abteilung* decided:

> The development of the situation in Africa urgently requires additional supply of modern and decisive weapons. Accelerated transfer of a *Tiger-Kompanie* (1/sPzAbt 501) to Africa has been ordered. The first elements of the company (six Tigers) were ordered to be transported starting on 10 November.

Following the Allied landings in northwest Africa on 8 November 1942, orders were revised to ship the unit to Tunisia. Due to delays in Tiger production, *schwere Panzerabteilung* 501 was still in the process of equipping. It had been issued two Tigers in September and eight in October along with 25 PzKpfw III Ausf N with the 7.5cm KwK L/24 gun. The remaining ten Tigers were issued in November.

The first three Tigers of the 1 *Kompanie* were unloaded from the ship *Aspromante* at Bizerte on 23 November 1942. The rest of the Tigers were shipped by loading one per motorized lighter. The next Tiger was landed at Tunis on 27 November but the rest were sent to Bizerte and landed as follows: two Tigers on 1 December, one on 6 December, one on 13 December, four

Far left
The transport of PzKpfw VI Tiger tanks to North Africa was a lengthy operation. A Tiger Ausf E from sPzAbt 501 (tactical number 112) fitted with wide combat tracks is loaded on an Italian ferry at the port of Reggio Calabria. (Schneider)

Positioning a Tiger on the cargo deck was difficult due to limited space. Parked on the dockside is a PzKpfw III, a PzKpfw VI Tiger along with other vehicles from sPzAbt 501 awaiting shipment. The ferry has been armed with a 2cm Flakvierling quadruple gun for anti-aircraft defence. (Schneider)

The Tiger tank was always a source of interest to the people of Tunisia. However, since a unit would be expected to operate over an expanded combat zone, actual combat effectiveness was limited. Usually only a few Tigers would be available for an attack on a specific target. (Schneider)

on 25 December, five on 8 January, one on 16 January, and the last two on 24 January 1943. Not a single Tiger was lost in transit! The cause of the delay in shipping the Tigers from *2.Kompanie/schwere Panzerabteilung* 501 to Tunisia was that it had been diverted to occupy southern France.

The *Stabskompanie* (headquarters company) had two *Panzerbefehlswagen* Tiger (command tanks) and five PzKpfw III (7.5cm L/24), and each *schwere Kompanie* (heavy company) was issued with nine Tigers and ten PzKpfw III (7.5cm).

As elements of units landed in Bizerte and Tunis, they were rapidly organized into ad hoc *Kampfgruppen* and quickly sent out to stop the British and US units driving eastward to occupy Tunisia. The commander of the *schwere Panzerabteilung* 501, Major Lueder, given command of one of these *Kampfgruppen*, wrote the following combat report dated 16 December 1942 on the initial actions with Tigers in Tunisia:

The first Tigers of the *1.Kompanie/schwere Panzerabteilung 501* were loaded on board a ship at Reggio Calabria (Italy) on 21 November. The *Abteilung* commander, Major Lueder, flew in advance to Tunis on 22 November and upon arrival was assigned command of a *Kampfgruppe* until his *Abteilung* arrived. On 4 December, he again took over command of the elements of his *Abteilung* that had arrived, which up to then had been led by *Hauptmann* Baron von Nolde until he was wounded, and then by *Leutnant* Vermehren.

Up to 1 December, four Tigers and four PzKpfw III had arrived in Tunisia. On 1 December, three Tigers and four PzKpfw III were operational. One Tiger was out of action due to problems with the engine.

After being assigned security tasks, the Tigers were moved to an assembly area 7km east of Djedeida. The order to attack came at 13:00 hours, and the Panzers immediately started toward Djedeida to gain contact with the oncoming enemy tank force moving northwestward. At 15:00, the Panzers encountered the first enemy activity, weak infantry forces 3km northwest of Djedeida. The *Kompanie* was hit by heavy artillery fire from the heights north of Tebourba and also repeatedly attacked by aircraft. *Hauptmann* Baron von Nolde fell when an artillery shell exploded while he was walking toward a Tiger.

The attack was carried forward against enemy tanks in the olive groves 5km west of Djedeida. The field of view and the field of fire were very limited in the thick olive groves. Enemy tanks could only be fought at close range. *Hauptmann* Deichmann, who left his Panzer to obtain a better view, fell when hit in the stomach by a rifle shot. The Tigers were hit by General Lee tanks firing at a range of 80 to 100m. This resulted in deep penetrations, but the last 10mm of the side armour held. This proved that the armour was excellent.

Two General Lee (M3) tanks were knocked out at a range of 150m. Others were eliminated by the 8.8cm FlaK guns. The rest pulled back. At dusk, the Tigers pulled back to the original *Stützpunkt* and *Panzergrenadiere* took over the forward defense line. One Tiger had fallen out due to engine failure and remained in the olive groves. A PzKpfw III was dispatched to guard the Tiger.

Lessons: Although it was undesirable to send only a few Tigers into action, this was necessary due to the enemy situation and the shortage of our own forces. The approach march was engaged by enemy long-range artillery fire that could not be suppressed.

It is especially difficult to direct Panzers in combat in olive groves because the thick tree crowns restricted the vision of many tank commanders and gunners. An attacking Panzer is easily knocked out by well-sited dug-in defences. In spite of unfavorable conditions, the crews' trust in their Tigers has greatly increased because of the quality of the armour.

One Tiger and three PzKpfw III were operational on 2 December 1942. With two additional PzKpfw III from *Panzerabteilung* 190 attached, and accompanied by an infantry *Kampfgruppe*, the unit advanced westward from Djedeida to attack Point 186.4 east of Tebourba. Strong defenses were emplaced in the olive groves east of Tebourba. Four anti-tank guns, six General Stuart (M3/M5) light tanks, two American armoured halftracks (M3) and some trucks were shot up. Our own losses included three PzKpfw III, of which one was a total write-off. The infantry took over the defence line at dusk. The Panzers were pulled back to guard Djedeida.

Lessons: Combat in the olive groves was unavoidable because Tebourba is completely surrounded by olive groves except in the northwest. Close cooperation between the Tigers and escorting Panzers is necessary. The shortage

The Tiger-Fibel also contained Panzerbeschusstafeln, instructions on where to fire at any enemy tank classified as being difficult to destroy. Here the M4 Sherman is detailed, the black areas marks the part of the tank which can be successfully penetrated using different ammunition. Pz denotes Panzergranate, armour-piercing (AP) and HK for Hartkern, high-velocity armour piercing (HVAP) and HL for Hohlladung high-explosive anti-tank, shaped charge (HEAT). (Anderson)

31-Tonner m Pz Kpfw **M 4** (General Sherman)

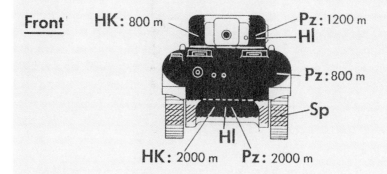

Front

HK: 800 m

Pz: 1200 m
Hl

Pz: 800 m

Sp

HK: 2000 m   Pz: 2000 m

Seite

Bei allen schwarzen Flächen
Pz: 2000 m
HK: 2000 m
Hl: Jede gefechtsm. Entfernung

Sp: Beschuß von Kette und Laufwerk

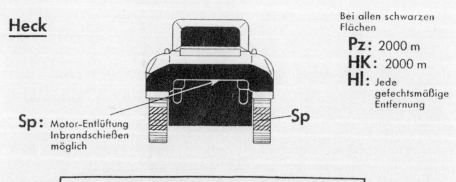

Heck

Bei allen schwarzen Flächen
Pz: 2000 m
HK: 2000 m
Hl: Jede gefechtsmäßige Entfernung

Sp: Motor-Entlüftung Inbrandschießen möglich

Sp

Die Angaben für diesen Kampfwagen sind errechnet.
Sie sollen als Richtwerte einen **vorläufigen Anhalt** geben.

28-Tonner m Pz Kpfw **M 3** (General Lee)

Front

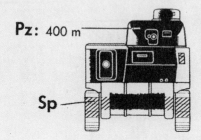

Pz: 400 m

Sp

Bei allen schwarzen Flächen
(außer Turmfront)

Pz: 2000 m
HK: 2000 m
HI: Jede
gefechtsmäßige
Entfernung

Seite

Bei allen schwarzen
Flächen

Pz: 2000 m
HK: 2000 m
HI: Jede
gefechtsmäßige
Entfernung

Sp: Beschuß von Kette und Laufwerk

Heck

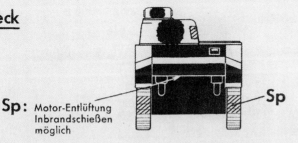

Bei allen schwarzen
Flächen

Pz: 2000 m
HK: 2000 m
HI: Jede
gefechtsmäßige
Entfernung

Sp: Motor-Entlüftung
Inbrandschießen
möglich

Sp

Die Angaben für diesen Kampfwagen sind errechnet.
Sie sollen als Richtwerte einen **vorläufigen Anhalt** geben.

The US-built M3 General Lee was included in this listing of enemy tanks as being difficult to fight. However, the prime advantage of this tank was the 75mm gun, designed to fire HE and AP shells, a benefit for the Allied tank crews. The armour on an M3 could easily be penetrated by any German tank gun, including that of the Tiger. (Anderson)

of command resources makes itself felt, especially the missing *Befehlspanzer* and the resulting lack of communication with the next higher command.

One Tiger and two PzKpfw III were operational on 3 December 1942. The unit again attacked toward Point 186.4 along the combat route taken the previous day. The Panzers were engaged by enemy artillery and mortar fire from positions on the heights that could not be spotted. In addition, they were attacked by aircraft. Three anti-tank guns, a mortar position, and three ammunition carriers were destroyed.

A Tiger was hit in the area of the final drive by an enemy 7.5cm self-propelled anti-tank gun. It was sent back to the starting point because its ability to remain operational appeared questionable. Both PzKpfw III carried the attack further forward up to the olive groves southwest of Point 196. The unit took up a "hedgehog" formation, remaining in the olive groves overnight. Several infantry losses occurred due to the bitter fighting by scattered enemy troops. At 03:00, the order was received to disengage from the opponent. The Panzers returned

A PzKpfw VI Tiger is carefully loaded on to a Marinefährprahm (MFP), a landing craft. More than 700 of these rugged and versatile vessels were built. The maximum carrying capacity of the vessel was just sufficient for the weight of a 65-ton Tiger tank. (Anderson)

to Djedeida, taking along the wounded and dead. Another anti-tank gun and an ammunition carrier were destroyed on the return march.

Lessons: The lessons of the previous days were confirmed. When fighting in close terrain with limited visibility, close cooperation with infantry forces is necessary, especially when attacking through woods.

Maintenance on the vehicles was performed on 4 and 5 December. This was difficult and time consuming because of the absence of the *Werkstattkompanie*.

Three Tigers and four PzKpfw III were operational on 6 December 1942. Three additional Tigers were being repaired. Before dawn the Panzers moved within 4km east of El Bathan and into El Bathan by 10:30. The commander of the 10.Panzer-Division, *Generalleutnant* Fischer, personally gave the orders to take the heights east of the pass west of Tebourba and to engage the enemy artillery thought to be located on the other side of the pass. The objective was reached without encountering any enemy activity. The enemy battery did not fire and therefore could not be spotted. The units turned south and pushed forward to the *Fallschirmjäger* (Paratroops) attack on Point 145 from El Bathan. Fleeing enemy columns and tanks were observed as soon as the Tigers appeared. The enemy could only be engaged with difficulty, because the hilly terrain constantly provided cover for the opponent. Point 145 was secured and attempts were made to gain contact with *Kampfgruppe* Gehrhardt, who were expected from the southeast. One Tiger was hit on the idler wheel and road wheels by an enemy 7.5cm self-propelled anti-tank gun. However, it remained drivable. From covered positions on the heights northwest of Medjerda, medium enemy batteries fired at the Tigers without success. The territory that had been gained was secured for the night in cooperation with the *Fallschirmjager* that had arrived.

Lessons: The morale effect on the Tiger crews was especially noticeable on this day. Without problems the Tigers easily managed the march through mountainous terrain.

On 7 December 1942, the Tigers were pulled back to an area 1km south of El Bathan. The *Kompanie* was assigned tactically to *Panzer-Regiment 7*. (*Kampfgruppe* Gehrhardt).

On 8 December 1942, the Panzers had to move to slightly higher terrain because the ground was no longer crossable due to persistent rainfall.

On 9 December, both Panzers (one Tiger and one PzKpfw III) arrived that had taken part in the march from Bizerte to capture and disarm the Ville navy base. It rained throughout the day. At 20:00, attack orders came in for the next day.

On 10 December 1942, five Tigers and four PzKpfw III were operational out of the seven Tigers and five PzKpfw III. Near Massicault, the unit joined the formation of *Panzer-Regiment 7*. Two Tigers were assigned to the lead company, the rest followed in reserve behind the main body of the *Kampfgruppe*. The objective was Medjez el Bab. Movement was restricted to the road conditions, the ground being too soft because of rain. Enemy resistance was first encountered 8km southwest of Furma. From hull-down positions, enemy tanks fired at the lead Panzers. One Tiger shot up two Stuart (M3/5) tanks and four armoured (M3) half-tracks. The advance continued 6km short of Medjez el Bab, the Panzers came under fire from several enemy gun batteries. The column took up defensive positions. The plan was to continue the attack after the *Panzergrenadiere* arrived and to advance on Medjez el Bab from the north on both sides of the river. During the approach march, the enemy tanks that had been driven off assembled in the high ground north of Furma and attacked our artillery positions. The Tigers, which were immediately sent to the rear, encountered 20 to 25 Stuart (M3/5) tanks and shot up twelve without suffering a single loss. Additional enemy tanks were knocked out by elements of *Panzer-Regiment 7*. The night was spent on the road from Furma to Medjez el Bab.

On 11 December 1942, the captured territory was mopped up by *Kampfgruppe* Gehrhardt. The Tiger took over defensive positions facing south against reported enemy tanks. Only several enemy armoured cars were spotted; they immediately pulled back. At 20:00, orders were received to pull the Tigers out and send them to a base 7km east of Djedeida at the disposal of the Army.

Lessons: If only a few Tigers are available, it is entirely suitable to incorporate the Tigers into a Panzer advance. Two Tigers assigned to the lead, served as battering rams and drew fire from dug-in defensive weapons that were difficult to spot. The rest of the *Kompanie*, following along in reserve, was to engage any threats expected to the flanks from enemy tanks. Tigers may not open fire too early against enemy tanks, in order to keep retreating enemy tanks within the effective range of our weapons for as long as possible. Tigers can maintain the convoy speed of the lighter tanks without reaching or exceeding the ordered limit of 30kph. The previous methods used in employing Tigers in Tunisia were the result of the prevailing conditions. We should strive for deployment of pure Tiger formations including their escort tanks as the *Schwerpunkt* (Spearpoint).

Seven of the eight available Tigers were operational on 16 December 1942. On 17 December 1942, Major Lueder also wrote the following report on the effectiveness of enemy heavy weapons and the usefulness of their own heavy weapons:

I. Enemy weapons:
A. Enemy tanks: The 7.5cm gun of the M3 (General Lee) could not penetrate through the Tiger's armour at a range of 150m. The last 10mm of the side

Above
Tiger number 142 ready for shipment. The narrow transport tracks are fitted to allow loading in the restricted cargo space of an MFP. The turret has been turned and the ball mounting for the hull machine gun (MG) has been covered. (Anderson)

Pages 124/125
Two Tigers from sPzAbt 501 roll past a forward radio post. Despite some concerns, the Tiger performed well in the foothills of the Atlas Mountains. (Schneider)

armour held up against a hit on the side armour that had been guarded by the sheet metal fender over the track.

The 3.7cm gun of the M3 (Stuart) is apparently very accurate. Fire was especially heavily directed at the driver's visor, commander's cupola, and the gap between the turret and hull. In one case, a shell fragment jammed the turret, temporarily taking the Tiger out of action. It is proposed that a deflector channel be added like those installed on the PzKpfw II and III.

B. Enemy anti-tank guns: At a range of 600 to 800m the 3.7cm and 4cm anti-tank guns penetrate through the front and side of the hull of the PzKpfw III. They succeed only in damaging the Tiger's road wheels and tracks, which did not result in immobilizing the Tiger.

In one case, at an estimated range of 600 to 800m, a self-propelled 7.5cm anti-tank gun hit a Tiger on the right front by the final drive. The Tiger was out of service temporarily due to the resulting failure of the weld seam.

C. Enemy artillery: Up to now only minor road wheel damage has been caused by shell fragments. Most hits on the Tiger were to suspension components, causing high wear on the road wheels, rubber tyres, track links, and track pins. Jamming of the interleaved road wheels has not occurred, and no Tigers were immobilized.

II. Our weapons:
A. The 8.8cm KwK gun is very accurate. Up to now, the Tiger has fired only at the M3 (General Lee) at ranges of 100 to 150m. The front and side armour were cleanly penetrated. The M3/5 (Stuart) was shot through at all ranges. We should strive to supply the Tigers solely with *Panzer-Kopfgranaten* (tracer shot) for better observation of each shot. An enemy battery was engaged at a range of 7,600m by using a gunner's quadrant. The enemy battery was silenced after six shots were fired. It is proposed that the *Tiger-Kompanie* be outfitted with a *Feldfunksprecher f* (field radio set "f") to enable forward observers to direct fire. In addition, the inverted-image rangefinders should be exchanged for converging image rangefinders. Large errors result from using the former type in terrain with no discernible landmarks.

B. The 7.5cm KwK (Kurz) has proven to be very successful in engaging mass targets with *Sprenggranaten* (high-explosive shells). The effectiveness of the *Hohlgranate* (shaped-charge shell) has not been established, because up to now only the Tigers have fought with enemy tanks.

After further minor actions in December and early January, the *Stab* and 1/sPzAbt 501 were sent into action in support of *Kampfgruppe* Weber, as detailed by Major Lueder on 27 January 1943 in his combat report for the period from 18 to 22 January 1943:

On 15 January, the *Stab* and *1.Kompanie* with nine Tigers and 14 PzKpfw III were attached to *Kampfgruppe* Weber. The *Kampfgruppe* had been ordered to attack

Far left
The gun barrel on this Tiger Ausf E has been covered with camouflage netting during a stop for the crew to purchase food from a local Tunisian. By 1943, Allied air superiority had become overwhelming for the German forces fighting in North Africa. (Kadari)

by circling past the right of the opponent who was pushing east toward Division Superga and to restore the situation by striking into the opponent's rear.

On 18 January 1943, two *Panzer-Kampftruppen* each with two Tigers and two PzKpfw III were attached to *Gebirgsjaeger-Regiment* 756, which was to open the passes east of Djebel Masseur at the beginning of the operation. The rest of the five Tigers and ten PzKpfw III as *Panzergruppe* Lueder were positioned south of Pont du Fahs (along with the *II/Panzergrenadier-Regiment* 69, two *FlaK-Kampftruppen*, a light *Flakzug* and a SdKfz 9 from *Panzer-Pionier-Bataillon* 49) ready to pursue and breakthrough in the rear of the opponent.

At 05:30, in close cooperation with *II/Gebirgsjaeger-Regiment* 756, the *Panzer-Kampftruppen* started engaging anti-tank guns and gun positions as well as bunkers that were very cleverly built into the mountain slopes. Toward 11:00, the left-hand *Kampftrupp* came to a halt because a further advance on the main road was prevented by a mine barrier watched over by heavy supporting fire. It was cleared after employing an additional three Tigers and three PzKpfw III as well as the armoured *Pionierzug*. After tough fighting, the top of the pass was reached at around 18:00.

Losses were, one Tiger from the destruction of the suspension components and damage to the transmission caused by hits, one Tiger by a jammed transmission, and two PzKpfw III due to hits on the suspension and driving onto mines.

Approaching 21:00, after regrouping the *Panzergruppe* advanced forward and despite enemy resistance reached the road fork southwest of the Kabir Pass at about midnight.

The Panzers destroyed heavy anti-tank guns and took in 62 prisoners. On this day, the *Panzerpioniere* lifted over 100 enemy mines.

The Tigers of sPzAbt 502 were supported by PzKpfw III tanks. Here a PzKpfw III Ausf N mounting the short-barreled 7.5cm KwK L/24 forms part of the column. The vehicles were used for scouting, supply purposes, and for protecting the heavy tanks against enemy anti-tank troops. (Schneider)

Experience: Without exception, the Panzers were kept to the roads and could be employed only as battering rams or to provide covering fire for the infantry moving forward on both sides. Clearing the mine barrier and the breakthrough could be accomplished only by the closest coordination and continuous personal exchange of ideas with the infantry battalion commanders.

The strong armour as well as the actual and morale effect of the 8.8cm KwK gun was especially advantageous during the difficult mountain fighting.

On 19 January 1943, after a short strike toward the southwest on the main road leading in the direction of Rabaa and as a follow up guarding this road with two *Flakkampftruppen*, a *Panzergrenadierezug* and the *Pionierzug/Panzerabteilung 501*, *Gruppe* Lueder started south in the following formation: two Tigers, two PzKpfw III, an armoured *Pionierezug*, a *Panzergrenadierekompanie*, the rest of the Tigers and PzKpfw III, and the main body of the *Panzergrenadiere*. The attack flowed smoothly forward after opening a gap that had been blocked by anti-tank guns and mines. The surprised opponent found no time for a serious attempt to effectively block the road. Resistance first increased in the afternoon. Two Tigers were immobilized by mines at a mine field guarded by anti-tank guns. The objective for the day, the crossroads near Bir Montea, was reached at 19:00. Approximately 25 guns (anti-tank and artillery) and 100 motor vehicles of all types were destroyed or were ready for collection by following elements. Some 100 prisoners were taken.

Experience: a Tiger drove through a mine barrier, without being damaged, while the following Tiger set off a mine even though it was driven exactly in the tracks of the leading Tiger – a lesson that even following the tracks in mined terrain does not offer absolute security. The effect of the mine on a Tiger is more or less heavy damage to the suspension, depending on the type of mine. In no case was the armoured hull penetrated. Personnel losses did not occur due to mines.

On 20 January 1943, in the same formation as on the previous day, the *Kampfgruppe* advanced toward the east against the gorges near Ousseltia and opened these with *Panzergrenadiere* riding on the Panzers. Beyond the gorges, contact was established with the Italians coming from the east. One Tiger became stuck by attempting to drive through a wadi. After regrouping, at around 17:00 the advance started south from the crossroads continuing in bright moonlight while continuously fighting the enemy until 03:00. The opponent very cleverly pulled back from ridge to ridge while laying numerous mine fields that he guarded with anti-tank guns and artillery. Often the last elements of the motorized mine layers were captured. The following combat methods were employed: Two Tigers advanced followed the armoured *Pionierzug*, then the rest of the Panzers. If the first Panzer hit a mine barrier, all of the rest of the Panzers immediately drove right and left to build straight platoon fire fronts and suppressed the anti-tank guns and artillery by suddenly opening fire. Under this protective fire, the *Pioniere* cleared the minefield while halted on the road; the *Panzergrenadier-Bataillon* provided flank security by firing from the vehicles. The area west of Djebel Halfa was reached at around 02:00, where security was set up toward the east and west in order to prevent the encircled opponent from breaking out or bringing up reinforcements.

A PzKpfw VI Ausf E Tiger in service with 2/sPzAbt 501, tanks from the 2nd company can be easily identified by the extra track links fitted to the front plate. More than 20 "Jerrycans" containing petrol are stacked on the roof of the turret. (Topfoto)

Experience: The Tigers were decisive even for the success of the night advance because mines did not cause any substantial damage. The well-positioned enemy anti-tank guns guarding the minefields, opened fire first, did not penetrate the Tiger's armour. At night and under continuous enemy action, minefields frequently were not recognized in time. Therefore, often the lead Tiger drove onto the mines and was immobilized – even if only for a short time. Result: The more Tigers, the better the advance flows.

On 21 January 1943, *Gruppe* Lueder secured the front line by establishing bases with anti-tank and anti-aircraft guns facing west and *Panzergrenadiere* facing east. The Panzers were held available behind the centre. On 21 January, an enemy tank assembly area was spotted near Ousseltia containing 60 tanks and a similar number of armoured half-tracks. The opponent advanced on a wide front toward the left-hand base of the *Gruppe*, but suddenly stopped his attack before coming within combat range. Maybe he intended to lure us out of our positions with this maneuver. When this failed, toward evening and during the night, individual combat vehicles advanced and were knocked out.

On 22 January 1943, with a force of 25 tanks followed by armored half-tracks, the opponent conducted an attack, at 16:00, against our right-hand

Stützpunkt but was brought to a halt 100m in front of our lines. Repulsing this attack was conducted under unfavorable conditions because the low-lying sun and dust clouds ruined the visibility. Therefore, only a few kills were achieved. The opponent used the following combat tactic: Advancing forwards on a wide front, he left the main body at a range of 2,000m, to show the opponent the widest side and to open fire.

After the attack failed, the opponent pulled back to the west as night fell. With limited Panzer counterstrikes on the flanks of the opposing force, and continuously switching the Panzers from one to the other *Stützpunkt*, plus the significant combat dedication of the PaK and FlaK crews, we managed to fool the opponent about our strength so that he again pulled back to the area of Ousseltia on 23 January and employed only artillery and aircraft in increasing numbers. For two days the *Kampfgruppe* had to endure long artillery barrages, often for many hours, and numerous bombing and strafing aircraft attacks. Two 8.8cm FlaK, three 2cm FlaK, and additional heavy weapons of the *II/Panzergrenadier-Regiment* 69 were knocked out by enemy fire. Two PzKpfw III were knocked out (of which one was a total loss). One Tiger was immobilized by a hit and burned out when it pulled back out of action. However, it could be towed back behind our own lines.

On average three Tigers and eight to ten PzKpfw III were operational each day during this period. The demands made by previous marches through the mountains and the damage caused by mines started to become noticeable in the Panzers. On 22 January, an attempt by the French to break into the rear of the *Kampfgruppe* was repulsed by the *II/Panzergrenadier-Regiment* 69. On 22 and 23 January, 20km further north, the opponent temporarily blocked the supply route, whereby several officers, NCOs and men fell into the hands of the enemy. The road was again reopened by a newly attached company from *Panzerabteilung* 190. In the afternoon of 23 January, connecting up with the Italian *Brigade* Benigni, which had advanced through Mansouf, was completed.

After the Italians took over the new main battle line under the protection of *Gruppe* Lueder, the *Gruppe* disengaged the opponent during the night of 24/25 January and moved to the area east of Mansouf. Having fulfilled all objectives, the *Gruppe* was disbanded on 25 January.

From available records, during the period from 18 to 25 January the *Gruppe* captured or destroyed: 25 guns, nine self-propelled guns or armored half-tracks, seven tanks (General Sherman, Lee, Stuart), about 125 vehicles, and two armoured cars. A total of 235 prisoners were captured of which eight were officers.

Experience: The Tigers have proven to be outstanding even during marches and combat in the mountains. However, all now need a complete overhaul and inspection. The fact that only one Tiger out of nine was still fully operational and two or three others were conditionally operational at the end of the operation should not be ignored. The time it will take to repair them will be governed by the possibility of performing the work needed. The lack of towing

Pages 132/133
A PzKpfw VI Ausf E Tiger of sPzAbt 505 has broken through a wooden bridge. The heavy tank is about to be towed onto firmer ground by another Tiger. After the first snow falls in late 1943, tanks were hand painted in winter camouflage by the crews. Note the large air filters, which are fitted to the rear of the hull. (Kadari)

Tigers operated by Panzerersatzabteilung (PzErsAbt – training and replacement units) were often fuelled with liquefied coal gas due to the shortage of petrol. A Tiger Ausf E tank from PzErsAbt 500 based at Paderborn has four gas bottles mounted on the engine deck. Paderborn was close to the manufacturer Henschel in Kassel, so technical support for the unit was readily available. (Münch)

equipment, the necessary dispersal of the workshop and repair sections as well as the transport of repair parts makes this difficult to achieve. Also it is vital that the still missing elements of the *Werkstattkompanie* and supply column of the *Abteilung* are rapidly shipped to Tunisia.

Details of the next action, which resulted in a Tiger falling into enemy hands, was reported on 3 February 1943 by Major Lueder, in the following combat report for the period from 31 January to 1 February 1943:

The *Abteilung* with eleven *Tiger-Gruppen* was attached to *Kampfgruppe* Weber, which had been ordered to restore the situation in front of Division Superga by a pincer-type attack to the south from out of the area south of Lake Kebir. Half of the Tigers were assigned to each of the two encircling groups.

The right-hand *Gruppe* under the command of *Hauptmann* Pommee, commander of the II/*Panzergrenadier-Regiment* 69, with six *Tiger-Gruppen* under the command of *Oberleutnant* Leese, as well as two *FlaK-Kampftruppen* and a *Pionierzug*, had to advance on the main road toward Robaa. The main body of the Tigers was to cover the *Panzergrenadier-Regiment*'s turning movement on the far side of the crossroads.

The left-hand *Gruppe*, under Major Lueder, was made up of the I/*Gebirgsjaeger-Regiment* 756 and five *Tiger-Gruppen* under the command of *Oberleutnant* Kodar, as well as two *Flak-Kampftruppen*. They were to advance south on the mountain road (similar to the action on 19 January), take the crossroads 18km south of Kebir Lake, and then cover the attack of the main body of the *Gebirgsjäger-Regiment*.

In accordance with orders, the right-hand *Gruppe* started out with the *Tiger-Gruppen* on point, reaching El-Hamra at 06:30, and came up to our own forward lines by Feriana without encountering enemy resistance and crossed our forward lines at 07:00. From here on, heavy enemy artillery fire from both sides struck the route of advance. The lead platoon drove through the sunken track near Point 431 while the enemy artillery fire became heavier. The lead platoon encountered mines, which were cleared away personally by the platoon leader, *Leutnant* Weber. Shortly after, two Tigers were hit under their guns, so that their ability to aim was hindered. In spite of this, the platoon proceeded further forward and again encountered a mine barrier. Because the terrain did not allow leaving the road and the previous lead platoon was already handicapped in its ability to fight, another platoon consisting of one Tiger and two PzKpfw III was ordered forward. Under their protection, *Pioniere* were to clear the mine barrier. The platoon passed through the cleared barrier and was advancing well when suddenly from the left several anti-tank guns opened fire on them at close range. In the following order, the two lead Tigers and four PzKpfw III were hit, which resulted in their being knocked out of action and in some cases to burn.

The crew of a Tiger Ausf E from sPzAbt 502 dressed in the standard black Sonderbekleidung für die Panzertruppe (special uniform for the armoured corps). The factory new tank is painted in standard dark yellow and is fitted with six smoke grenade dischargers on the turret. A further six are mounted on the top of the hull. (Münch)

The Panzer crews took up positions on the ridge somewhat to the rear and provided covering fire for the dismounted attack by the *Panzergrenadiere*. However, the attack of the *Panzergrenadiere* could not make headway against the prepared defensive system in the deeply rutted and mined terrain. The Italian artillery employed in the same sector could not shoot because of trouble with telephone lines. With the aid of the *Panzerkompanie*'s radios, they commenced fire with good effect at 16:00. The tanks repulsed the opponent's scouting patrols that were apparently sent to recover one of the knocked-out Tigers. The lead Tiger burned fiercely from the moment it was hit. Because it was not possible to tow it out, it was blown up after dark. We managed to tow out the second knocked-out Tiger in spite of the continuous enemy defensive fire.

Destroying the lead Tiger which stood within the enemy lines was unavoidable. Before it was blown up, the opponent did not manage to recover anything out of the burning Tiger. One officer, three NCOs, and eight men were missing from the crews of the knocked-out Panzers. They were either killed from the hits and the resulting fires in the Panzers or were captured by the enemy after they bailed out.

On orders from the Division a security group, consisting of one Tiger and two PzKpfw III as well as a *Panzergrenadierkompanie* remained on 1 February to provide security for disengaging with the opponent as well as recovery of the second Tiger. This *Gruppe* was also pulled back to the ordered assembly area during the night of 2 February. The Panzers destroyed one self-propelled anti-tank gun, four additional anti-tank guns, one armoured car, several machine-gun nests and scouting patrols.

A Tiger Ausf E from sPzAbt 505 loaded on an SSyms railway wagon for transport away from the front in the late summer of 1943. Barbed wire has been fixed to the sides of the hull by the crew to prevent Soviet close-combat teams climbing on the tank. Two running wheels are missing, an indication of the heavy fighting which occurred around Kursk. Although strictly forbidden, the tank has still been loaded on combat tracks. (Anderson)

Back in the East

On 31 August 1943, Major Gomille, commander of III/PzRgt *"Grossdetuschland"*, reported on the combat of his Tigers:

Pages 138/139
Infantrymen advance covered by a Tiger Ausf E, possibly from sPzAbt 502. In the background a wooden hut is burning, during the war both sides destroyed any buildings which could serve as cover for their enemy. (Münch)

14 August 1943

Battalion headquarters was situated in the wood 2km southeast of Jassenowoje. Around midday the marching grouping of the last transports arrived at HQ.

Detraining point:	Nizhniy Ssrirovatka
Distance to bttn. HQ:	110km

General condition of the *Abteilung*:
Strength

Staff company:	Three Tiger command tanks
	Three APC of the reconnaissance unit,
	w/o ordnance
10.Kp.:	complete (One Tiger still in Germany)
11.Kp.:	Four Tiger destroyed during rail transport with
	the bulk of the workshop equipment
9.Kp.:	No operational Tiger
Missing:	The staff and the workshop companies also all
	the wheeled vehicles for the staff company.

By the evening of 14 August 1943 was ready for action

Three Tiger command tanks
13 Tigers from 10.and 11.Kp.
-----
16 Tigers

Ten Tigers broke down during the march from Nizhniy Ssrirovatka to battalion headquarters due to minor and serious damage. Already the loss of the complete supply train, the workshop, the recovery section and all spare parts became noticeable. In the following days the absence of these support elements, which are vital for any tank unit, became even more critical…

15 August 1943

At a 04:00 meeting of the commanders at Jassenovoje. The divisional Ia (chief of the staff) leads a combat group consisting of:
PzRgt *"Grossdeutschland"* Tiger Abt, I.Abt, One Panther Kp.), One AufklAbt(mot) (motorized reconnaissance battalion), II.(Sfl) (*Selbstfahrlafette*) ARGD (self-propelled artillery).

Mission: Advance via Grun and Budy to Belsk, destruction of penetrated enemy forces. Fall in at 05:30, in the following order:

A PzKpfw VI Tiger Ausf E from sPzAbt 505 ready for action during the winter of 1943. The tactical number 101 is painted in white, usually brighter colours were used to differentiate the tanks. The thick mud on the running gear is a sign of the unpredictable rise and fall of temperatures found during a Russian winter. (Anderson)

Ahead the only Tiger Abt followed by the IAbt (PzKfw IV), then the Panther Kp, both the latter had the task to protect the flanks of the Tiger Abt…

The *Tiger-Abteilung* advanced on both sides of the road towards Grund. At 1km north of Grund the tanks received heavy fire from AT guns. The enemy guns were destroyed after a short firefight. Only a short time later the leading Tiger ran over a mine, but was only slighty damaged… The rest of the *Abteilung* turned left now and approached two deep transverse ravines, which were difficult to cross. The bulk of 10.Kp halted to provide protective fire, while 11.Kp pushed the advance further. While crossing the ravines, the Tigers received fierce fire from extraordinarily well camouflaged AT guns and T-34 assault guns. After a longer firefight this enemy was completely destroyed. *Hauptman* von Villebois, commander of 10.Kp was severely wounded. His tank received eight direct hits from 12.2cm shots (T-34 assault guns). Six rounds hit the turret, three of them causing smaller dents and two double palm-sized chips. The hits disabled the electric firing mechanism… one hit penetrated the hull, the metal was severely distorted causing the weld seam to crack over a length of 50cm, making a repair within the troop impossible.

After reaching the cemetary the *Abteilung* turned right, entered the village and destroyed the two T-34 assault guns then advanced to the southern outskirts of Grund without any noteworthy resistance.

The *Abteilung* now had six Tigers operational, including two command tanks (one tank was lost due to mines, the rest disabled due to mechanical damage)…

The northern edge of Budy was tenaciously defended by AT and AA guns. The enemy was annihilated at no own losses… The tank assault was ferociously supported by II/Rgt ARGD (Sfl).

Losses:

Personnel:	One dead, one severely wounded, six wounded.
Material:	Six Tiger damaged by enemy action
	Seven Tiger by mechanical damage (engine, gearbox and gun)

Successes:	21 AT, AA guns and other guns,
	Eight tanks and assault guns,
	One scout car totally destroyed…

18 August 1943

The Division received orders to advance from Achtyra vua Kaplunovka, Parchomovla to southwest to contact the SS units in position there.

For the attack the PzRgt (Tiger Abt and IAbt, *2 Pantherkompanie*) was reinforced by I.(SPW)Bttl. PzGrenRgt GD (armored infantry) and II/Regt ARGD (Sfl) (self-propelled artillery). The *Tiger-Abteilung* will launch a first

In the summer of 1944, the sPzJgAbt 653 was issued with a Porsche Tiger equipped as a command tank. The Tiger (P) was fitted with a machine gun (MG) and additional armour. The vehicle has been coated with Zimmerit anti-magnetic paste. Note the opening in the hatch on the cupola to allow signal flares to be fired by the commander. (Münch)

attack to break through the first Russian positions in order to gain the important heights 3km northeast of Michailovka...

When the Tigers reached their positions, eight ran over mines. The mines were *Holzkastenminen* (wooden box mine) captured by the Soviets, under which one or two German 21cm grenades were placed to boost the explosive effect. The mines were placed close together and the tanks ran mostly over three to four mines at the same time. While the normal box mines caused only marginal damage, those reinforced with grenades caused more serious damage. Five Tigers received only slight damage and three broke down with severe damage.

Losses:
Personnel:	One wounded
Material:	Eight Tigers by mines

Successes: Five AT guns

Ready for action: By the evening four Tigers

19 August 1943

The four Tigers remaining ready for action were sent to the regiment under leadership of *Oberleutnant* Arnold... In combat against a strong Russian *Pakfront* (AT gun line), one Tiger is shot up by a T-34 assault gun (clean penetration of the upper hull). After annihilation of this AT gun position the assault proceeded against Parchomovka...

Losses:
Personnel:	Three killed, one wounded
Material:	One Tiger heavily damaged, two Tigers with gun damage

Successes: Twelve tanks, twelve heavy AT guns, six light AT guns

Ready for action: By the evening five Tiger

The *Tiger-Abteilung* of PzRgt "*Grossdeutschland*", reduced to only a handful of operational tanks and backed by a small combat group, was able to fight numerically superior Russian forces. The Tigers were deployed in textbook operations as *Rammbock* (battering ram), relying on their armour and weaponry. The regiment had other tanks, including a few PzKpfw IV to give flank protection and some Panthers to back the assault with their long-range high-velocity guns. A number of Tigers were lost, and many tanks were damaged by enemy fire or mines. The number of total losses appeared to be surprisingly low, most tanks could be repaired in the field or after being successfully recovered.

On the Soviet side the losses were atrocious. Within eight days the *Abteilung* destroyed 54 guns, 42 tanks as well as assault guns and eliminated a great number of soldiers.

New Russian Tanks

The Soviets never stopped development of their heavy tank, the KV-1 was continuously simplified, improved and refined. By 1943, the KV-1 that appeared on the battlefield was a "flattened" version which had an improved mobility due to less weight. Both armour protection and firepower (7.62cm gun) remained the same. This soon led to criticism, as the heavy tank did not offer a better performance than the T-34. By early 1944, the KV-85 was entering service.

In 1944, the Soviets Army introduced the upgraded T-34/85 (known to the Germans as the T-43) and the new JS-2 heavy tank in increasing numbers. Both tanks had powerful guns (85mm and 122mm respectively), with firepower similar to current German tank guns. The deployment by the *Panzerwaffe* of the PzKpfw IV and the *Sturmgeschütz III*, became problematic, it was not always possible to compensate for obsolete material with better combat tactics. The JS-2 entered the battlefield in summer 1944.

A Tiger Ausf E parked on the roadside for technical maintenance. In contrast, supplies are being moved by horse-drawn carts. German and Soviet forces both relied on this method of transport to a great extent. (Anderson)

The German HWA (Army Ordnance Bureau) noted:

I. New Russian tank "I.S." 122 (Josef Stalin)
A heavy Russian tank was destroyed in the south of the Eastern Front, which in all likelihood is the new, announced in various reports "Josef Stalin". A proof for this assumption is:

a. A shield fixed to the tank with the inscription
   I.S. 122 – Josef Stalin Kal. 122 mm
b. Directly before contact with the tank, Soviet POWs independently described and drew the tank, showing its characteristics accurately

The predicted maximum armour thickness of 250mm does not apply. Present measurements resulted in:

Technical data

Weight:		50 tons (estimated)
Dimensions	Length:	6.45m (without barrel)
	Width:	3.10m
	Height:	2.65m
	Width of tracks:	0.65m
	Ground clearance:	0.40m
Armour protection	Gun Mantlet:	100mm (maximum)
	Turret:	100mm (all around)
	Turret roof:	30mm
	Front:	100mm
	Sides:	90mm
	Rear:	60mm
	Hull roof:	30mm
	Bellyplate front:	30mm
	rear:	20mm
Ordnance:	122m gun with muzzle brake	
Length of barrel:	5,230mm (no muzzle brake)	
Calibre length:	L/43	
	One 7.62mm MG, DT right of the driver	
	One 7.62mm MG, DT in turret beside the gun	
	One 7.62mm MG, DT in rear of turret	
Observation means:	Three periscopes at driver's position	
(noted on the	One periscope in turret right of gun	
burned-out tank)	One periscope in cupola	
	One rotating periscope on top of turret left of gun	
	Six observation slits in cupola	

Engine:	12-cylinder diesel, mounted in the rear as in the 152mm assault gun

2.) Characteristics:

Turret as with T-34 located to the front, drop-shaped when seen from above, tapered to the rear.

Commander's cupola located at rear of turret roof, offset to the left.

Driver's visor in the centre of the front.

Suspension as with KV-1, six running wheels and three return rollers, drive sprocket at rear, idler wheel at front.

3. Combat against JS-2:

In general, the same conditions apply as for the KV-85, considering the Stalin has 30mm thicker armour at hull and superstructure.

a. PaK and KwK:

The notes for the KV-85 published in the new tank-combat charts dated 1 March 1944 can be adopted (so far published for 7.5cm PaK 40, KwK 40 and StuK 40 L/48).

With 7.5cm KwK 42, 8.8cm KwK 36 and 8.8cm PaK 43 the new tank can be engaged at ranges up to 1,000m at the strongest parts of the armour, at all other parts at ranges up to 3,000m and beyond (exception: sloped frontal armour in front of the driver). Indeed "*Nashorn*" (previously called "*Hornisse*") with 8.8cm L/71 achieved kills penetrating the turret front at ranges up to 2,600m.

"Tiki", was a famous Tiger Ausf E from sKp/SS-PzRgt 2 "Das Reich" and was named by the commander after his girlfriend or wife. Although the tank appears untouched, the crew has painted three kill rings on the gun barrel. (Anderson)

Axis infantry seek cover behind the rear of a Tiger Ausf E. Although understandable – the tank offered protection against enemy fire but this could become a deadly trap. On the battlefield, any Tiger attracted fire from every available enemy gun. Note the thin steel rope carried on the side of the hull to allow the crew to haul a track back on to the running gear. (Anderson)

b. Heavy infantry weapons and artillery:
Combat with the respective hollow charge round (constant penetration). When using HE rounds with PaK, KwK or FlaK infantry and artillery guns obstructive or destructive impacts can be achieved on optics, vision slits and suspension and by jamming the turret.

c. Infantry weapons (hand and automatic weapons):
Obstructive impacts can be achieved on optics, vision slits on the cupola, periscopes and open hatches.

Pages 148/149
A Tiger of sPzAbt 502 parked alongside a Soviet KV-1s (a lighter version of the KV-1) still armed with the older 7.62cm gun. Later KV-1s tanks were fitted with a larger turret mounting a 8.5cm gun, for combat against Tiger tanks. (Topfoto)

d. Close combat:
Beware of the turret rear MG and pistol plugs. A destructive impact can be achieved with shaped charges, *Faustpatrone* and *Panzerschreck* (RakPzb 43), and by cleverly attaching anti-tank-mines or *geballte Ladung* (bundle of hand grenades)

Only a short time after the JS-2 was encountered on the battlefield, comparative tests with German tanks began. Soon a comparison between German tanks and the new Soviet T-34/85 and JS-2 was published by *Waffenamt Prüfwessen* 6 in Hillersleben. The *Panzeroffizier* at the Chief of General Staff compiled a similar note:

Comparison of German PzKpfw vs. Soviet PzKpfw T-34/85 and JS-2
The penetration data for the following German PzKpfw guns

Panzer IV	with 7.5cm KwK 40
Panther	with 7.5cm KwK 42
Tiger I	with 8.8cm KwK 36
Tiger I	with 8.8cm KwK 43
Tiger II	with 8.8cm KwK 43

...was compared to those on the new Russian PzKpfw T-34/85 and JS-2. Since no test firings were conducted, all penetration data referring to these was calculated. The calculations were based on appendix 2: Assembled armour strengths and angles of slope.

The Russian 85mm KwK (L/51) fires an AP round with a projectile weighing 9.2kg at a velocity (Vo) of 792m/s, and the Russian 122mm KwK (L/45) an AP round with a projectile weighing 25.6kg at a Vo of 800m/s. The penetration data was taken from Russian documents. Data was available only for ranges up to 2,000m; the data for ranges up to 3,500m had to be estimated. Below the penetration data for 100m range and armour sloped at 60°:

7.5cm KwK 40 with 7.5cm PzGr 39	99mm
7.5cm KwK 42 with 7.5cm PzGr 39/42	138mm
8.8cm KwK 36 with 8.8cm PzGr 39	120mm
8.8cm KwK 43 with 8.8cm PzGr 39/43	202mm
85mm KwK (r) with 85mm PzGr (r)	10mm
122mm KwK (r) with 125mm PzGr (r)	134mm

The calculations were based on an assumed angle of slope of 60°. The steel quality was put on the same level as our armour for the tests, for cast steel a 14 per cent lower plate strength was projected. The hit probability was neglected with this comparison. Roughly estimated it can be stated that the

Panzer IV
Is far inferior to both the T-34/85 and the JS-2

Panther
Is far superior to the T-34/85 at frontal fire, and roughly equal at side and rear; and superior to the JS-2 at frontal fire, and inferior at side and rear

Tiger 1 with KwK 36
Is superior to the T-34/85 and inferior to the JS-2

Tiger 1 with 8.8cm KwK 43
Is far superior to the T-34/85 and superior to the JS-2

Tiger 2
Is far superior to both the T-34/85 and the JS-2

This report shows that the Germans did not succumb to any illusions, all shortcomings of their tanks armed with 7.5cm KwK including StuK were clearly revealed. Even the Tiger Ausf E was considered rather ineffective, especially if the main armament was firing AP rounds. The suggestion that the situation with the Tiger Ausf E would improve when mounted with the 8.8cm KwK 43 is of academic interest only, since this gun never entered service on the Ausf E. Although the Tiger Ausf B wins, when judged from the tactical point the Ausf B certainly fails because the excessive weight of the tank seriously limited mobility. It appears that in this comparison the PzKpfw V Panther (by German standards a medium tank) remains as the best all-round tank. However, it should not be forgotten that the JS-2 mounted a much more powerful gun (two calibre classes) at approximately the same weight.

1944

After the disaster at Stalingrad and the failure of Operation *Citadel* in 1943, the German forces had lost the initiative. On the Eastern Front Soviet forces overcame the numerical weaker German forces, which were pushed back in heavy defensive battles. The year 1944, brought bloody battles culminating in Operation *Bagration*, which led to the collapse of the entire *Heeresgruppe Mitte* (Army Group Centre). The superiority of the PzKpfw VI Tiger Ausf E diminished. The Soviet military had learned quite a number of tactical

Dry shelter was a rare luxury at the Eastern Front. Whenever the situation allowed, troops erected improvised sheds. Although these Tigers of sPzAbt 501 are parked in deep mud, they are protected against rain and snow which made the task of maintenance crews much easier. (Münch)

Above

In the summer of 1944 the Soviet-built IS-122 (JS-2), which was a development of the KV heavy tank, appeared on the battlefield. Armed with a 122mm gun and with thick frontal armour, the heavy tank was able to fight on equal terms with the Tiger Ausf E. This JS-2 was destroyed by tanks from sPzAbt 506. The inscription on the turret states: "Destined for OKW" (supreme command of the army). (Anderson)

lessons, and could rely on their endless resources in human beings, and output from their factories. Since mid-1943, weapons were available to successfully defeat German heavy tanks.

The German forces were still able to win battles. And the Nazi propaganda machine still operated. The demoralized German population created a phrase: *Wir siegen uns zu Tode* – We win until Death. Panzer troops won a number of battles, but they failed to win the war.

The situation on the Southern Front in Italy, and even more so on the Western Front in France after the D-Day invasion was vastly different. Beside having a massive superiority in weapons and troops, the Allies fought using the same strategies and tactics, as German invaison forces did in 1940.

The battlefield qualities of the Tiger were superbly demonstrated on the Eastern Front, where the Germans could rely on better combat tactics and superior weaponry. It has always been a marvel to the author where this fighting spirit (or was it courage born of despair?) originated.

The same isolated combat by Tiger tanks, which proved so successful in the East, became useless when fighting the Allied forces employing equally as good tactical skills, backed by air superiority.

A captured Russian soldier was interrogated by officers of 98.PzAufklKp on 28 January 1944:

The company was issued with ten factory-new T-34 tanks fitted with Russian 9 RM radio (improved version), waveband 160 to 225m.

By 25 January, three tanks were sent on a reconnaissance mission to Sosovka. Returning crews told that all three T-34 were shot by Tiger tanks.

On the night of 27 January, the remaining seven T-34s, reinforced by tanks of an unknown unit (total 20 tanks) launched a reconnaissance mission to the west. In the dark the tanks lost contact. At dawn five tanks gathered at a wood NE of Ssob station. At around midday a Tiger appeared and shot up all tanks…

Such incidents deepened the respect for the Tiger tank.

The sPzAbt 502 remained subordinated under AOK 18 in 1944.

From an after action report of Major Schwaner, commander of sPzAbt 502, dated 19 August 1944:

Subordination relations:
Staff company, 2/ and 3/sPzAbt 502 are subordinated under 38. Army Corps, 1/sPzAbt 502 will be subordinated under 50. Army Corps from 23 June 1944.
Situation:
On 22 and 23 June 1944, the enemy penetrated the main line of resistance to a width of 2km after an artillery barrage of 60 to 80 batteries (approximately 300 guns)

Alarm and mission for sPzAbt 502:
On 23 June, at 20:00 3/sPzAbt 502 is alerted in their accommodation at

Left below
The cast front armour of the JS-2 has received a number of direct hits from 8.8cm KwK 36 tank guns. Apparently none have penetrated. Some indentations made by shells, which have ricocheted off, have been marked in white by astonished German tank crews. The lowest hit on the hull was fired from a Tiger at a range of 1,200m, the upper at a range of 1,000m. (Anderson)

This diagram from a German Panzerbeschusstafel (leaflet for anti-tank combat) for the 8.8cm KwK 36 shows the weak points on the verstärkt (uparmoured) KV-1 which entered service in early 1943. The leaflet differentiates between Hartkern (HK – HVAP) and Panzer (Pz – AP) shots, although the former was available only in limited amounts. When the more powerful KV-85 and JS-2 tanks appeared, the Germans did not update the leaflets, all documents referred to the later KV-1. (Anderson)

44-Tonner s Pz Kpfw **KWIC** (verstärkt)

Front

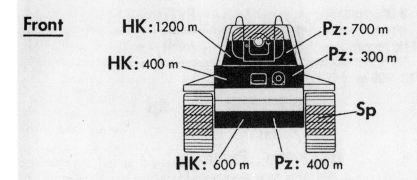

HK: 1200 m
HK: 400 m
Pz: 700 m
Pz: 300 m
Sp
HK: 600 m
Pz: 400 m

Seite

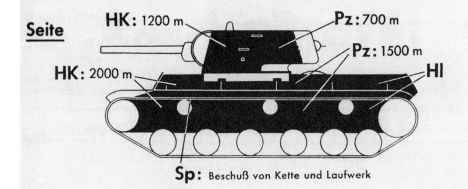

HK: 1200 m
Pz: 700 m
Pz: 1500 m
HK: 2000 m
HI
Sp: Beschuß von Kette und Laufwerk

Heck

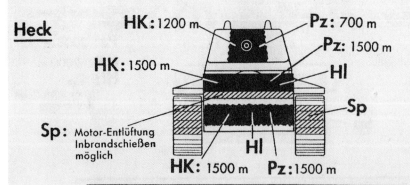

HK: 1200 m
Pz: 700 m
Pz: 1500 m
HK: 1500 m
HI
Sp
Sp: Motor-Entlüftung Inbrandschießen möglich
HI
HK: 1500 m
Pz: 1500 m

Die Angaben für diesen Kampfwagen sind errechnet.
Sie sollen als Richtwerte einen **vorläufigen Anhalt** geben.

Rubinjati. Later the staff and 2/sPzAbt 502 march together to Pyldai to launch a counter attack to recapture the old main line of resistance. The companies reach their destination during the course of the night after 30km travel on roads with few losses. Tanks ready for action: 1/sPzAbt staff company one *Befehlswagen* Tiger, 2/sPzAbt ten out of 11 Tigers, 3/sPzAbt 11 out of 14 Tigers…

The assault position of 1/sPzAbt and 2/sPzAbt 502, shows that the *Abteilung* had an action readiness of more than 85 per cent. The counter attack on the Sujevo hill was launched at 07:30, 24 June 1943. The Tigers of 2/502 succeed in breaking through the enemy lines, but are forced to a halt since supporting infantry came under heavy artillery fire. To the right, Pioneer Battalion 121 exploits the situation, and supported by 3/sPzAbt 502 mounts a thrust deep into the enemy line which succeeds. At 11:00, the company had reached Voschtschinino where GrenRgt 94 and 2/502 can now utilize the situation to proceed with their attack. The Soviet forces (three infantry regiments and parts of a tank brigade) are shocked by the bold pincer attack. By 12:00, 2/sPzAbt and 3/sPzAbt 502 reach the Soviet trench system, and meet heavy resistance. The trench system is impassable to tanks. In rapid succession many enemy bunkers, machine gun and grenade launcher positions also a number of tanks ambushed in the village of Sujevo can be destroyed by the gunfire of Tiger tanks. Only elements of the Soviet forces could be chased out of their positions, the majority offered brisk resistance. The supporting German infantry had also suffered heavy losses. Due to the extreme heat of the summer day, men were exhausted and could only manage to catch up with the tanks in the evening. Tigers were sent back to boost the morale and collect up whole infantry platoons. Still standing in front of the Soviet positions, the Tigers repelled three counter attacks destroying seven tanks and hundreds of enemy troops. Now the Soviet artillery fired on this sector oblivious to the danger of hitting their forces. Two Tigers were damaged and one had to be abandoned on the front line. Since the German infantry was not able to overwhelm the dug-in Soviet forces at Sujevo, both Tiger companies were withdrawn by 22:00.

Although the counter attack did not achieve the objective, the Tigers were able to destroy a great number of enemy tanks and artillery. The after action report of sPzAbt 502 ends this day with the following entry:

Results

Enemy losses:	20 tanks (T-34 and KV-1)
	Five AT guns
	Two enemy infantry battalions destroyed
Own losses:	Two Tiger tanks, one on the front line
Dead or injured:	None

The following German counter attacks were initially more successful. The enemy lines could initially be penetrated until terrain conditions worsened, the recent rains had filled the many craters and remnants of the Soviet trench systems creating deep muddy holes. The report carries on:

An officer inspects the hull machine-gunner's position on a Tiger Ausf E from sSS-PzAbt 103 (part of sPzAbt 503). The tank is coated with Zimmerit anti-magnetic paste which was applied to all tanks from mid-1943 to mid-1944. (Anderson)

...The Tigers can only advance gradually and the commanders have to brief one another. Two days before the attack a heavy artillery barrage began... pounding the enemy artillery does not always succeed. The concentrated enemy artillery fire from anti-tank guns and 15.2cm assault guns take their toll among the Tigers. The company *Hauptman* von Schiller reports two Tigers hit and immobilized, as does *Leutnant* Carius...

The village of Suijenov, which lay on the old front line, cannot be taken completely. Despite this the attack on Sujevo continued and the Tigers of Carius and von Schiller had to support the infantry as they occupied the old trenches. Again the report:

...The Tigers come under heavy fire. One Tiger of the Carius group was destroyed by artillery and assault guns, after succeeding to destroy two assault guns at a range of 1,500m. Two further Tigers of the von Schiller group are immobilized. To avoid further losses while passing over the top of the hill, all Tigers are withdrawn to reverse-slope positions for anti-tank defence or any counter attacks by the enemy ...The positions to the east of the hill can now only be taken by

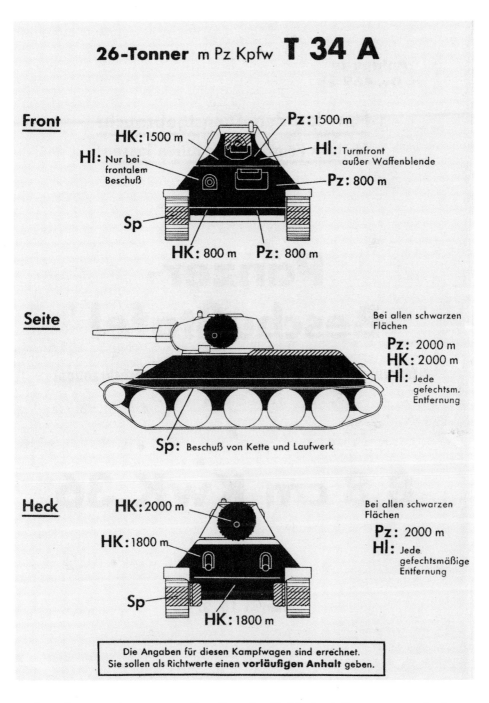

26-Tonner m Pz Kpfw T 34 A

Front

HK: 1500 m

Pz: 1500 m

Hl: Nur bei frontalem Beschuß

Hl: Turmfront außer Waffenblende

Pz: 800 m

Sp

HK: 800 m   Pz: 800 m

Seite

Bei allen schwarzen Flächen

Pz: 2000 m

HK: 2000 m

Hl: Jede gefechtsm. Entfernung

Sp: Beschuß von Kette und Laufwerk

Heck

HK: 2000 m

HK: 1800 m

Bei allen schwarzen Flächen

Pz: 2000 m

Hl: Jede gefechtsmäßige Entfernung

Sp

HK: 1800 m

Die Angaben für diesen Kampfwagen sind errechnet.
Sie sollen als Richtwerte einen **vorläufigen Anhalt** geben.

The Tiger-Fibel contained Panzerbeschusstafeln for many enemy tanks. Unlike the KV heavy tank, which evolved into the JS series, the armour on the T-34 was not increased to a similar extent. (Anderson)

the infantry under support of artillery. By 13:00, the infantry managed, after suffering heavy losses, to occupy the old front line…

By 15:00, the enemy launched a counter attack with seven tanks (KV-1 and US-supplied Sherman) supported by 400 infantrymen. *Hauptman* Leonhard's Tigers destroyed two KV-1 heavy tanks. The enemy infantry succeeded in throwing back the Pioneers positioned on the forward slope of the hill... It was not until nightfall that something like calm was restored... In total nine Tigers were immobilized on the main battle line by artillery and anti-tank gun fire. During the night, all remaining Tigers were deployed to recover damaged tanks. By the morning of 27 June, five Tigers had been recovered.

Results

Enemy losses:	Two 15.2cm assault guns, destroyed
	Two KV-1, destroyed
	Four 12.2cm AT guns, several medium AT guns and
	SP guns destroyed by fire or overrunning, 500 casualties
Own losses	Seven Tiger tanks immobilized, five were recovered
Dead or injured	Nine

Over the next two days further attacks were launched. Finally Sujevo was taken the old front line was re-established. The report of sPzAbt 501 summarises:

...The *Abteilung* launched a successful attack with a staff and two companies in cooperation with an infantry regiment and a pioneer battalion. This attack

Tiger "233" from sPzAbt 507 is coupled to an SdKfz 9 with two rigid tow bars by a recovery team. A machine gun is mounted on the cupola, in preparation for any attack by patrolling enemy aircraft. The unit badge, featuring a blacksmith forging a sword, is visible on the front plate of the hull. (Anderson)

stopped the enemy advance and led to the recapture of the old front line... The combat was to cost both sides an enormous expenditure of infantry, tanks and artillery. Temporarily the Soviets had the advantage of a battle for the control of one fortified height...

The attack was possible only with the support of Tigers, without them there would not have been a success. We lost some Tigers due to direct hits by enemy artillery and assault guns. It was extremely unfavorable that during the attacks on 24 June and 26 June, the Soviet force could easily observe the entire terrain from the north. This could have been avoided by launching further attacks to the north to eliminate this threat. The infantry and artillery forces necessary for such an attack were not available.

At the end of the battle, sPzAbt 502 had to write off three Tigers as total losses, of which two had to be destroyed by German forces. A further six tanks were recovered and repaired. Two armoured half-tracks were damaged, but were recovered and repaired.

A Tiger Ausf E from sPzAbt 502 ploughing a track though the deep mud of the Eastern Front, early in 1943. The track guards have been torn off and the air filter system is completely missing. (Hoppe)

Pages 160/161
At least three Tigers from sPzAbt 502 advance and provide cover for members of the infantry. The commander of each tank has closed the turret hatch for safety. (Topfoto)

Hungarian tank crewmen get trained to operate the Pzkpfw IV, StuG III and Tiger. Germany supported the Hungarian Army by supplying heavy equipment and munitions. The Tiger is from sPzAbt 503 and after training the unit handed over ten tanks to the Hungarian Army. (Kadari)

Right
A Famo SdKfz 9 heavy tractor being used to haul a disabled Tiger Ausf E of sPzAbt 505 on to a SSyms railway wagon. Loading a heavy tank was a difficult procedure. After loading the SdKfz 9 would simply be driven off the side of the wagon. (Anderson)

In the September 1944 issue of the bulletin of the *Panzertruppe* an after action report of an (unknown) Tiger company was published:

...the Tiger company had the order to clear the enemy, who managed to infiltrate, out of the woods and then to continue the attack. At 12:15, the attack by the Tiger company began supported by an infantry battalion. The dense wood allowed only 50m vision, the narrow path forced the Tigers to march in a single line. The Soviet infantry quickly escaped from their positions when the Tigers advanced. All anti-tank guns, which had been positioned within an hour or so after the start of our attack, were quickly defeated. A number of anti-tank guns were destroyed by direct hits, others were overrun. A lot of guns were captured intact.

After the frontal platoon managed to advance 2km into the wood, the platoon leader observed chopped-down trees and a large muzzle brake (Josef Stalin) directly in front of him. He immediately gave the orders "AP round! Telescopic sight! Fire!" At the very same moment his Tiger was hit by two 4.5cm rounds, obscuring his sight. In the meantime a second Tiger of the platoon approached his position. Despite limited vision he opened fire at a range of 3,500m. The Josef Stalin tank retreated behind a low hill. Meanwhile the second Tiger took the lead. It fired three rounds at the enemy tank. After the third shot the Tiger was hit by a 122mm round, fired directly at the front. The AP round

A Tiger from sPzAbt 505 photographed in the spring of 1944. By that time the unit had changed to a new marking system, the tactical number being stencilled on the gun housing. The badge of the Abteilung, a charging knight, was painted on the sides of the turret. It was still common practice to carry long wooden planks or tree trunks. The apertures for a telescopic gun sight have been covered with a piece of cloth to protect the lenses from frost. (Anderson)

A Tiger from sPzAbt 505 photographed through the driver's vision visor. The thin steel cable carried on the side of the hull was used to haul a track back onto the sprockets. The front outer running wheel is missing. (Kadari)

did not penetrate, probably because it hit the Tiger at an unfavourable angle. Then the enemy tank was put out of action by a round perforating the gun barrel. A second Josef Stalin tank rose up and tried to give cover for the first, which tried to withdraw. During a short shooting match one of the Tigers hit the second Josef Stalin under the turret. The round penetrated and set the tank on fire. The rate of fire from the Josef Stalin was comparatively low.

The company leader reported some experiences learned from this short battle against Josef Stalin tanks:

1. As soon as Tigers advance, the Josef Stalin tanks turn and try to avoid a shooting match.
2. In most cases Josef Stalin tanks engage in shooting matches only at long range (beyond 2,000m), or if they succeed in moving to favourable positions (edge of a wood, localities, ridges).
3. Enemy crews tend to leave their tank after receiving a first hit.
4. In most cases the Russians tried to recover or blow up bogged-down Josef Stalin tanks at any price, to avoiding it falling into our hands.
5. The Josef Stalin tank can be destroyed, even without being able to penetrate

the heavy frontal armour (Another *Tiger Abteilung* had reported that the frontal armour can only be penetrated at ranges below 500m).

6. One should always try to get onto the flank or the rear of the Josef Stalin tank, in order to destroy it with combined fire.

7. A shooting match with Josef Stalin tanks should be commenced only in platoon strength. Any combat by a single Tiger will lead to its loss.

8. After the first hits, it proved to be favourable to blind the enemy crew by firing HE rounds.

The *Generalinspekteur der Panzertruppen* (Inspector General of the Armoured Troops) gave some remarks (extracts):

No. 4 ...A disabled Tiger must never fall into enemy hands! This basic principle has to be performed by any crew member with dedicated commitment.

No. 5 and 6 When attacked by 12.2cm tank guns and 5.7cm AT guns in the east and the 9.2cm AT/AA gun in the west and southwest the Tiger cannot

Photographs were always important for soldiers. Only the sitting soldier wears the complete reversible winter uniform. The black and white image gives an idea of how good this camouflage suit worked. (Anderson)

rely on armour alone. The basic combat tactics have to be obeyed as it is for all other tanks.

No. 7 This conclusion is correct; but three Tigers may not retreat when facing five Josef Stalin tanks, only if they are not in platoon strength. The combat by tank vs. tank is all too often decided by the better tactics.

No. 8 In this context it shall be noted that Josef Stalin tanks can be defeated on the flanks or from the rear not only by Tiger tanks, but also by PzKpfw IV and *Sturmgeschütze.*

This report reveals some interesting aspects. Even in 1944, German tank forces had a considerably better level of tactical skills. Speaking of the classic tank vs. tank combat the Soviets were vastly inferior, in spite of the installation of radios and improved tactical training.

The fact that the Inspector General of the Armoured Troops suggests to fight the Josef Stalin tank with inferior tanks (PzKpfw IV and *Sturmgeschütze*) by simply attacking them from the side or rear certainly appears to have been cynical.

By 22 July 1944, sPzAbt 502, at that time equipped with Tiger Ausf E, met the JS-2 in greater numbers for the first time, Major Schwaner noted in his report dated 19 August 1944:

Leutnant Bölter attacks Leikumi by 11:00 meeting strong resistance 500m southeast of the town. Here the enemy had placed eight tanks and several AT

guns to protect his southern flank. Six T-43 and several trucks with towed AT guns are destroyed. During the further advance two Tigers are immobilized by enemy fire…

By 13:00, the 2.Co. surprisingly meets 20 medium and heavy tanks (T-43 and JS-2). *Leutnant* Carius, being ahead of his company with three Tigers, immediately attacks on the move. His three tanks destroy 17 enemy tanks at close and very close ranges. He shot up ten tanks, only three are able to retreat to the east…

A Porsche Befehlstiger, tactical number 003, from sPzJgAbt 653. The turret has been turned to the rear. The tank carries powerful radio equipment, essential for a command vehicle. Note the two radio aerials. (Münch)

Successes:	23 tanks (17 T-43, six Josef Stalin), six heavy AT guns
Own losses:	Two Tiger immobilized by AT or tank gun fire
Losses:	None

The report continued.

On 23 July, two T-43 tanks and three AT guns destroyed without any losses. On 24 July, 17 tanks destroyed, *Leutnant* Carius and another man severely wounded. On 25 July, 18 tanks, five AT guns destroyed without any losses. On 26 July, twelve T-43 tanks and one JS-2 tank, 19 AT guns also 34 trucks destroyed. Own losses, two Tigers and three killed.

Over the period of 10 July to 26 July, the sPzAbt 502 destroyed 84 enemy tanks, one assault gun, 71 AT guns, two artillery guns and 1,250 enemy soldiers. Own losses are summed up as three Tiger Ausf E destroyed, ten Tigers immobilized (all recovered and repaired by the workshop). Three men were killed and 28 were wounded.

A total of 555 AP rounds of 8.8cm PzGrPatr 39, 876 HE rounds of 8.8cm SprGrPatr and 36,000 rounds of 7.62mm MG ammunition were fired.

The workshop company was able to repair 49 Tiger Ausf E over this period of 16 days and returned all to combat. There were never more than 28 combat-

ready tanks available. The lowest number was seven (12 July). At the end of this period, only twelve Tiger Ausf E tanks were serviceable in the *Abteilung* from the original allocation of 32. The authorized strength was 45.

sPzAbt 503 in Hungary

In October, 1944, the sPzAbt 503, now equipped with the PzKpfw VI Ausf B (*Königstiger* – King Tiger), was deployed to Hungary. After a short demonstration of power at the castle of Budapest the unit was ordered for

A Tiger Ausf E from sPzAbt 503, tactical number 334, parked between some farm cottages in a Russian village. Such a position offered a hiding place for the tank and accommodation for the crew. (Münch)

immediate action at Debrecen east of the river Theiss, where the situation had worsened. The armoured elements were entrained towards Szolnok. Due to shortages of SSyms wagons, the Tigers had to be transported by road on heavy trailers. Immediately after unloading, the tanks were all moved to the assembly areas. The tanks which arrived the next day were combined in another combat group. The commander commented:

> …The *Abteilung* saw combat in two groups under the command of different units. Their mission was to attack and advance into the enemy's rear. Both combat groups were extraordinary successful. From 19 October 1944, until the unit reformed on 23 October a total of 120 AT guns and 19 howitzers were destroyed. The stubborn enemy (a penal battalion) was shocked by the unyielding attacks, his rear echelons were shattered by the destruction of several transport columns and a supply train. The complete route of combat

Above
Tigers parked in a field, covered by a sparsely wooded ridge. In combat it was essential to position infantry on the ridge to guard the tanks. (Kadari)

Left
An SS officer in the cupola of a PzKpfw VI Tiger Ausf E. The hatch, which opened outwards, was secured when closed by three latches. (Anderson)

A late production Tiger Ausf E of sSS-PzAbt 102 is driven down a track in a French forest, during July 1944. The tank is being followed by a Famo SdKfz 9 heavy tractor. The crew has fitted extra track to the glacis plate to reinforce the armour. (Anderson)

(250km) was covered without any major mechanical breakdowns. In these battles the Tiger II Ausf B has performed remarkably well regarding armour, armament and mechanical reliability. Tanks receiving up to 20 hits without breaking down were not a rarity…

…By 31 October, the *Abteilung* rolled in the Kecskemet region to intercept Russian spearhead forces heading towards Budapest. In most difficult, partly swampy ground unsuitable for tanks breakdowns promptly occurred, mainly drive sprockets, tracks, idler wheels and engine coolers. Spare parts were ordered, but did not reach the *Abteilung* in time. This led within a short time to the bulk of the *Abteilung* becoming unserviceable. Due to missing recovery equipment the *Abteilung* had the choice to either blow up broken down Tigers, or to tow them back using other Tigers. Quite naturally mechanical problems arose with those tanks used for recovery. Only thanks to well organized and timely entrainment the *Abteilung* were to avoid greater losses of tanks.

The few intact tanks were now sent from division to division. Tasks were given which were impossible to achieve… Since 18 November, the *Abteilung* has been in combat in the Gyöngyös area. The enduring very poor weather made

leaving paved roads impossible. Since both armoured infantry and infantry units are too weak, the Tigers and even the *Flakpanzer* have to fight on the frontline without any close infantry support. We continuously received orders to take a town at night, in un-reconnoitered terrain and with far too weak infantry assistance... Such attacks are only successful when the *Grenadiere* participate alongside and in front of the Tigers destroying the concealed AT guns, which cannot be fought by the tanks. Sadly, they retreat at the first sign of enemy resistance leaving the Tigers alone, making them targets for enemy AT teams.

The Soviets tended to concentrate heavy AT gun batteries behind the front line. Fortunately only two Tigers were hit by the American-supplied 9.2cm taper-bore AT guns [also Soviet 100mm and 57mm AT guns]. These guns can penetrate even the gun mantlet at ranges under 600m. Penetrations at the rear of the turret will cause the ammunition to explode resulting in a total loss.

In combat, the 8.8cm KwK 43 is destructive at ranges up to 1,500m against all enemy tanks including the Stalin (JS-2). In favorable conditions the T-34

Above
Four Tigers from PzAbt 505 in the winter of 1943. All tanks have been painted with whitewash. All the crews wear the reversible winter suits, but showing the "summer" (dark) side. (Anderson)

Left
In the West all German forces were vulnerable to attack by Allied aircraft. Woods and built-up areas proved to be a perfect place to hide and wait for the enemy to arrive. (Anderson)

and T-43 can be destroyed at ranges up to 3,000m. We discovered quite often that, as happened in the east, the Soviet tanks avoided direct contact with our Tigers, or turned away after the loss of the first tanks.

In summary it can be stated that the Tiger B has proven itself in every aspect, making it a formidable weapon feared by the enemy. The Tiger unit, put into combat in numbers and used in a tactically correct way will always bring a resounding success. However, most superior authorities will not listen to the technical and tactical needs of a *Tiger-Abteilung*.

Two whitewashed mid-production Tiger Ausf E carefully camouflaged at the edge of a wood but if necessary, ready for immediate action. The tank carries the tactical number 1 and is coated with Zimmerit, anti-magnetic paste. (Anderson)

This report shows that concentrated combat of the battalions (according to the combat principles) was rather the exception than the rule. The thin German line had to be reinforced by whatever unit was available. Remnants of tank and infantry divisions were merged to *Kampfgruppen* (combat groups). If Tiger units were available, these were formed into platoons, and often enough a single tank was sent into action. Following another basic principle of German tactics, these *Kampfgruppen* were used for counterattacks. Although they were surprisingly successful, the captured territory could never be held. The German strength was as ever, too weak.

In some after action reports from Tiger units and German infantry commanders, some leading officers of combat groups had overrated expectations.

This dramatic report shows the reality of the late war fighting. In the east, German armoured forces were numerically too weak to defend the vast frontline. The same applied to the infantry and other support units also supposed relief divisions that existed only on paper. Despite great and impressive successes in counterattacks, the German units including the *schwere Panzerabteilungen* were never able to hold the ground taken and retreat was the order of the day.

Another after action report by Alfred Rubbel, at that time *Leutnant* and commander of a Tiger B in sPzAbt 503 underlines this point. The combat history of this unit was analyzed after the war by members of the Austrian military academy:

...in the early morning of 21 April 1945, a Soviet tank formation of 20 tanks breaks through the German lines west of Altruppersdorf. The Soviets overran the headquarters of 13.PzDiv (renamed PzDiv FHH 2 after its annihilation

By the end of July 1944, the 3/sPzAbt 503 had been re-equipped with Tiger Ausf B and positioned at the old French garrison town of Mailly-le-Camp. The Abteilung suffered many losses after the D-Day invasion. (Panzerfoto)

Pages 182/183
A Tiger Ausf E from SS-PzRgt 2 "Das Reich" photographed during Operation *Citadel* in 1943. The tank shows the "Mephisto" marking and the Kursk marking stenciled on the front plate. (Topfoto)

at Budapest) and advance further to the west. *Hauptmann* von Diest-Körber, the commander of sPzAbt 503, waiting at Altruppersdorf, is alarmed. His sPzAbt consisting of only five Tiger B, follow the Soviet advance. He reinforces his unit with some Wespe SP guns, which are positioned in a small village en route. Three further Tiger B, being returned from the workshop, join his unit, but only later. *Leutnant* Rubbel gets an order to scout the position of the Soviet tanks. After finding them, von Diest-Körber passes the order to deploy a wedge formation in order to attack. The unit takes position at the Mitterhof farm. Suddenly incoming fire strikes from a nearby forest. In a fierce battle the Tiger B of 503 destroy ten tanks (JS-2 and T-34/85) during the battle and a further eight during the chase at no own loss. A few more will be shot up by German AT guns as they crossed the narrow German lines to east.

The Austrian cadets came to the conclusion that the Soviet breakthrough was not part of a major offensive, but a decision made to use an opportunity. The high number of tanks destroyed is a sign that Soviet commanders underestimated the relative fighting strength and the determination of the German force.

Above
The sPzAbt 505 was re-equipped with Tiger Ausf B after the Soviet offensive during Operation *Bagration*. This vehicle was possibly photographed near Ohrdruf training site. (Clark)

Left
The Tiger Ausf B was fitted with the same type of cupola as used on the late production Tiger Ausf E. A metal sighting device was mounted on the front of the cupola, to assist the commander in passing target positions to the gunner. (Panzerfoto)

In the west, where the Allied armies conducted a much more sophisticated type of warfare, the situation was even worse. Wherever a tank assault was planned, a massed artillery barrage and air attacks by fighter bombers prepared the ground. German counterattacks were repulsed by this same type of action.

Unfortunately there are only few surviving after action reports dealing with Tiger B units.

This last combat was transcribed after the war. In 1945, *Unterscharführer* Diers was commander of a Tiger B of sSS-PzAbt 503, turret number 314, and his report details the last of the fighting in and around Berlin:

19 April 1945
We moved into an assembly position at Bülow near Seelow. A direct hit from a JS-2 on the turret damaged the cupola. Despite this defect, I destroyed 13 enemy tanks within 19 minutes by using the emergency trigger.

20 April 1945
To undergo maintenance we moved to Müncheberg, where the turret was repaired. During the welding work a fire broke out, which was dowsed by the Tetra extinguisher. Weapons and optics damaged.

21 April 1945
At night an alarm is caused by a Russian breakthrough. March to Berlin towing another damaged Tiger to Tempelhof, to the repair works of Krupp und Druckemöller steel company.

23 April 1945
Combat in Siemensstadt and Marienfelde.

24 April 1945
Early in the morning, marched to Neukölln and Köpenick over the Teltow-canal and destroyed a JS-2 on the bridge.

25 April 1945
The battle for Tiergarten begins. The Russians try to advance north via *Bergstrasse* and *Berlinerstrasse*. We move to the command post at *Potsdamer Platz*. However, the command post had already moved. Together with Tiger 100 (Uscha Turk) we cover *Potsdamer Platz*... Two further Tiger B are in combat at *Bahnhof Halensee*.

29 April 1945
One JS-2 and several T-34 tanks which had appeared from behind *Haus Vaterland* were destroyed. Due to its long chassis and barrel the JS 122 blocks the road as a massive obstacle...

30 April 1945

We are ordered to move to the *Reichstag* by the afternoon. The *Reichstag* has been severely bombed and is in ruins, the plenary hall has burnt down. Near the Kroll Opera House, we spotted 30 Soviet T-34. After a short briefing we rushed out of the cover of the *Reichstag* and open fire with good success. Many Soviet tanks were left burning…

1 May 1945

Five Tiger B of the *Abteilung* are still in combat. Near *Bahnhof Halensee* five Russian tanks are destroyed. We hold our position at the *Reichstag* while further Russian tanks go in position at the Kroll. We received the order to break out, allegedly this came directly from Goebbels. Three to five further tanks should join us. Our objective is Oranienburg in the north, were we shall close ranks with combat group Wenk… A short time later we learn that Adolf Hitler and Goebbels have committed suicide… Later in the evening, we decide to blow up the tank, and to leave Berlin.

Unterschaführer Diers and his crew survived this terrible battle and the war.

Left
A German engineer spray-painting camouflage on a Tiger Ausf B. Tactical number 300 identifies this vehicle as that of the commander of the 3rd Company. (Panzerfoto)

Below
The driver and wireless operator of this Tiger Ausf B of sPzAbt 503 wait for orders. The large dome under the gun barrel was a ventilator for the fighting compartment. Any direct hit an by anti-tank (AT) gun or even shell splinters would simply shear them off. (Panzerfoto)

Above, above right
After being withdrawn from the Western Front, sPzAbt 503 was re-established with 45 Tiger Ausf B. By October 1944, the unit had been transferred to Budapest where the Tiger Ausf. B was used in "psychological" warfare. The appearance of the heavy tanks from sPzAbt 503 helped to suppress a political coup, which would have enabled Hungary to negotiate an armistice. (Panzerfoto)

Left
US troops prepare to recover a damaged Tiger Ausf B in the autumn of 1944. A large white star has been painted on the turret in order to identify the tank as a captured vehicle. (US Signal Corps)

Pages 195/196
The end of the war in Italy. US infantry pass a disabled Tiger Ausf E. The drive sprocket is missing, but the track has been fitted over the road wheels to make the tank mobile. Clearly in this instance, Allied forces arrived before the Tiger could be recovered. (US Signal Corps)

Maintenance 7

It was not until the PzKpfw VI was deployed for combat in the desert of North Africa and on the Eastern Front that problems were found. Although each troop was able to cope with most technical shortcomings, at this early stage every combat operation became a risk. Many of these deficiencies could lead to a mechanical breakdown, followed by a recovery operation by specialist troops using heavy equipment.

The sPzAbt 501, in North Africa, was one of the first units to receive the Tiger Ausf E and equipped with 20 in two companies. Towards end of the fighting Major Lueder summarized his experiences in a field report.

Organization of the maintenance services:

One platoon of the workshop company was deployed stationary as a maintenance base. The facility must be carefully camouflaged and the platoon must be able to use the heavy lifting gear. Therefore firm ground is a basic requirement. Closed workshops are advantageous for major repairs, especially for welding works during the night. The so called "work tents" are only a poor expedient. The available twelve-man tents are unsuitable for Tiger maintenance. This workshop platoon will remain at its location until the recovery distances for heavily damaged Tigers become too long, or the unit is transferred to a remote combat sector.

The second platoon is deployed near the accommodation facilities of the Panzer companies as an emergency task force.

The maintenance services in combat:

At the begin of combat all maintenance services will be combined under leadership of a maintenance staff, which keeps in contact with the combat echelons via radio and motorcycle messenger. Maintenance troops will follow the combat echelons carrying the most important spare parts providing rapid repairs. To make these troops mobile, captured enemy APC (half-track vehicles) were used to best advantage.

Removing the turret of a Tiger Ausf E required heavy lifting equipment. Engineers from sPzAbt 504, use a mobile recovery crane mounted on a Faun L 900 for this task. The vehicle was normally not issued to a sPzAbt, which had to rely on the less mobile gantry crane. (Kadari)

A PzKpfw VI Ausf E issued to Panzerersatz und Ausbildungsabteilung 500 (PzErs-und AusbAbt 500), a training and education establishment based at Erlangen, near Nuremberg. Due to fuel shortages, the Maybach engine was modified to run on liquefied coal gas stored in four large pressurized bottles mounted on the engine cover. The tank is loaded on a Culemeyer SdAnh 121, the only flatbed trailer with a capacity of 65 tons. (Anderson)

The bulk of the maintenance services will follow with the supply column and comprise parts of the workshop also elements of the recovery platoon.

The less mobile parts of this emergency workshop platoon follow with the supply train as long as the combat situation and road conditions allow. The central spare parts storage is located here. It will be served from the storage at the stationary maintenance base by highly-mobile motor vehicles. In addition the remaining less mobile parts of the recovery section are located here.

In combat the easier repairs including damage to suspension and thrown tracks will be accomplished by the *Panzerwarte* (armour maintenance team) of the emergency task force. Simpler breakdowns to an engine or transmission will be repaired by specialists sent by the maintenance staff. Heavier damage, which can be repaired within a few hours without heavy lifting gear, will be repaired by a work team from the main workshop.

If the task requires heavy lifting gear, and if the Tiger is under fire, the tank must be hauled back to cover (if possible), where it will be safe to use cranes. The maintenance staff will follow the advance with the bulk of the maintenance services.

In a combat sector, where a Tiger is badly damaged, that cannot be held, the tank has to be towed back. At an absolutely safe place the repairs can take place, even if they take up to three days (replacement of engine, transmission, fuel tank or cooling system). If no spare parts are available, the tank must be hauled back to the stationary workshop. If there is a Tiger in the workshop with intact parts, it can be useful to remove the parts required and use for the damaged tank. Thus further haulage of the damaged Tiger will be avoided saving fuel, running wheels and time. The Tiger can then be returned to the battle.

Basic principle for the Tiger maintenance is:
1.) Maintenance at the place of the breakdown
2.) Storage of at least one spare engine and transmission

Assessment of the lifting gear:

The 15-ton gantry crane: On the Tunisian roads and even in the mountains the crane is easy to move. On curving mountain roads the driver must show extreme skills. Regarding lifting capabilities, the crane is perfectly suited for the stationary workshop platoon.

The 10-ton Faun crane: Has proven to be essential for repair work on the turret of a broken down Tiger in an off-the-road location. On firm ground the crane can be driven to any place. The steering system on the Faun is easily damaged. In the most difficult terrain it must be towed to the Tigers position by a half-track vehicle. This crane is the only equipment capable of lifting the turret of a Tiger, in case the 15-ton gantry crane cannot be used.

The 22-ton flatbed trailer can only be used on roads and firm terrain. As soon as the terrain becomes soft, usage of this trailer is not possible as it cannot be turned.

Signed: Major Hans-Georg Lueder

When it was necessary to replace a torsion bar, virtually all the running gear had to be removed. The extensive repair work being carried out on this Tiger Ausf E from sPzAbt 505 would certainly have kept this tank out of action for some time. Such heavy maintenance could only have been completed in an absolutely safe area, beyond the reach of enemy artillery or aircraft. (Kadari)

The *Nachrichtenblatt der Panzertruppen* published a short essay in the August 1943 issue:

...From the field report of a sPzAbt:

A Tiger broken down on firm ground, either on or off road, can be easily recovered by two prime movers (SdKfz 9). The Tiger will be connected by tow bars to the first *Zugmaschine*. It is powerful enough to tow the Tiger. Longer distances cannot be covered, since the weight of the Tiger pushes the prime mover off course. For this reason another prime mover has to be attached using steel ropes. Thus, the first *Zugmaschine* will be kept in the desired direction. It is important that both prime movers coordinate all movements. When towing a Tiger on mountainous roads with steeper gradient and descending curves it is necessary to restrain the tank with an attached heavy vehicle (a PzKpfw III is ideal). Otherwise the Tiger will push both prime movers sideways off the road. When the broken-down Tiger has lost a track, it is advisable to remove the other track to allow the tank to roll on its running wheels. Using this method, recoveries over distances of more than 100km have been successful. All instructions regarding the avoidance of damage to the transmission and brakes have to be strictly followed. A Tiger sunk in soft ground can be recovered by two prime movers standing on firm ground by using winching equipment. The unit succeeded in recovering a number of sunken Tigers by using a PzKpfw III. In emergency situations it was possible to recover a disabled Tiger under fire, regardless to any damage inflicted to the tracks or suspension, over distances of up to 3km with a PzKpfw III. However, this type should only be used for short-range recoveries, since the steering brakes on a PzKpfw III suffer serious wear. So far we have not been entirely successful in towing a disabled Tiger by another Tiger, since the required rigid towing equipment is not available. The towing points on a Tiger are useless. The tow bars for the prime movers do not fit the couplings on a Tiger...

The introduction of medium and heavy tanks required basic changes to the organizational structure of the workshop facilities. Each sPzAbt was issued with a *Werkstattkompanie* which was already in effect since April 1942.

Maintenance and recovery

From an after action report of a *Tiger-Abteilung* in Italy:

The mountainous region which was most unsuitable for tanks and the fact that we had to assist infantry forces resulted in requirements the *Abteilung* could not fulfill. A combined deployment was never achieved, and the combined action in company size was possible only three times. On the other hand a withdrawal of the *Abteilung* would have endangered this front section. Usage of a Tiger *Abteilung* in mountainous regions will remain the exception, but was necessitated by the situation.

Compared with other theatres of war more technical breakdowns had to be anticipated from the outset of the operation. If the recovery section of this unit

After attaching the special lifting cables, the turret of this Tiger Ausf E from sPzAbt 504 can be carefully removed. The "factory new" appearance of the tank, suggests that the operation is being carried out as part of a training exercise for both workshop and recovery crews. Note, the Tiger is fitted with the narrow rail transport tracks. (Kadari)

Pages 203/204
The Fries gantry crane had a lifting capacity of 15 tons. A Tiger Ausf E (912) of 3.SS-PzDiv "Totenkopf" has been reversed away so that work on the turret can begin. Note that the crane has been positioned at the edge of a forest to be hidden from reconnaissance aircraft. (Panzerfoto)

did fulfil all requirements, it was only possible by dedicated deployment and the personal commitment of all men in the platoon.

Some examples:

1. One Tiger became stranded in a ford with damage to the final drive. Although the cause of the break down had been located, the tank was recovered and hauled back to a workshop despite strafing aircraft and heavy artillery barrage.

2. During a tactical withdrawal, a Tiger broke down due to transmission failure. Early in the day, the recovery section hauled the Tiger through an abandoned village saving the tank from falling into enemy hands.

3. After the rescue of this Tiger, the section was ordered to recover a Tiger which had been damaged in action. When the three prime movers reached the location, the tank battle was still raging. Recovery took place under continuous attacks by fighter-bombers and a well-targeted artillery barrage. Both Tigers were towed back to our own lines. Another Tiger was recovered under similar circumstances.

The loading team has not followed strict orders in that the combat tracks on the Tiger must be replaced by the narrow tracks for rail transport. The latter could be carried on any SSyms wagon. (Anderson)

4. Several broken down Tigers had to be towed over a longer distance on a twisting mountain road. One prime mover received a direct hit from artillery, leaving three

seriously wounded and one dead. The recovery operation continued. A damaged bridge in a gorge halts the convoy. Troops worked hard to prepare a crossing. The tracks on the tank had to be flame-cut before it could be towed off the bridge by two SdKfz 9 prime movers. The operation had to be performed under steady artillery fire. An ammunition truck and a fuel bowser are hit and explode. After this action the prime movers had to be completely overhauled.

The second recovery section was called for, and the towing operation on the mountain road proceeded. Two further Tigers, which became stuck ahead of our own infantry, were recovered and moved some 8km back despite enemy AT, mortar and infantry fire. During the recovery one Tiger breaks through a bridge. All attempts to recover this tank failed, the Tiger was crippled by enemy fire and had to be abandoned. The Sapper section built an auxiliary bridge, so that two further Tigers could be evacuated. One 2cm *Vierling auf 8t Zugkaftwagen* (SP quadruple FlaK gun) and an APC (armoured half track) secured this operation. The twisting roads were successfully negotiated. The recovery section had to be used in daytime, since during the night the only suitable road was menaced by partisans or blocked by columns of troops and vehicles. Accompanying FlaK provided cover for all recovery operations against continuous dive bomber attacks, two kills were counted.

Routine maintenance for the Tiger tanks was an essential and continuous process. The maintenance crew was responsible for the tank and even followed the vehicle to the workshop, when heavy repairs were required. Here members of the maintenance crew clean and replace gaskets on the air filter system. (Schneider)

Recovery of a Tiger Ausf E or Ausf B from soft ground required up to five Famo sZgKw 18t (SdKfz 9) heavy tractors. An Ausf E from sPzAbt 503 is being towed to the workshop by two SdKfz 9 halftracks. The only visible damage to the tank is that two outer roadwheels are missing. (Rubbel)

The *Generalinspekteur der Panzertruppen* (Inspector General of the Armored Forces) commented this:

> These examples show that tanks can be recovered under worst conditions by deliberate deployment of recovery sections and unquestioned duty of all soldiers. In the fifth year of the war, any tank is precious, so this readiness must be demanded. The performance of these recovery sections has to be given the highest praise.

By 8 June 1943, the Inspector General of the Army published recommendations regarding the organization of the workshop units:

> The establishment of a workshop platoon with 52 men and 18 vehicles at the staff company of the Tiger battalion suggests a tripling of repair duties:
>
> Smaller damage will be repaired by the *Instandssetzungsgruppen* (workshop echelons) of the combat companies.
>
> Medium damage will be repaired by the *Instandsetzungsstaffeln* (workshop sections) of the staff company.

Heavy damage will have to be repaired by the *Panzerwerksattkompanie* (tank workshop company).

Mobile workshop sections will be established by the workshop company.

Major Schwaner, commander of sPzAbt 502 wrote this report dated 21 August 1944:

Technical field report for the period from 22 June to 10 August 1944

The *Abteilung* is equipped with PzKpfw VI Ausf E

The eight-week replenishment near Ostroff-Pleskau from the end of April until mid-June allowed an extensive maintenance programme, which included work which is not possible during combat. This included, general overhaul of the suspension, total cleaning of the cooling and fuel system, inspection and adjustment of the engine, transmission, turret drive and brake system. The spare parts situation was secured thanks to the long time of calm...

The deployment to the next combat took place by 22 June, during night and

This sketch from the Tiger-Fibel explains the correct method of recovering a Tiger from a river bed. Four SdKfz 9 heavy tractors are attached to two Tigers, enabling the bogged-down tank to be winched out. To the right, the sketch shows the correct method of towing a Tiger by two SdKfz 9 vehicles. (Anderson)

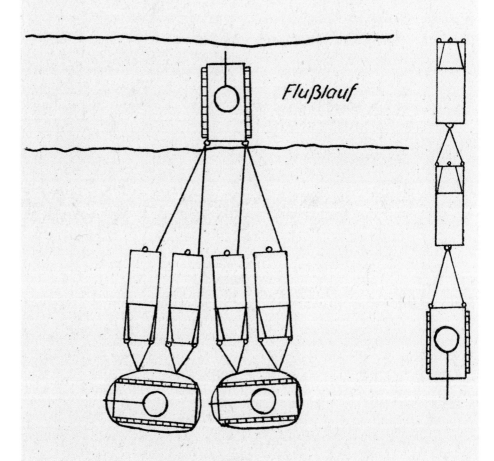

Motto: Mit Ruhe, Umsicht und Bedacht —
dann ist das Bergen bald vollbracht.

Genau, wie Du Deinem Kameraden in jeder Lage hilfst, mußt Du auch Deinen stählernen Freund wieder heimholen, wenn er liegen blieb.

Notfalls kann Dich ein Tiger-Kamerad flottmachen, aber vermeide es.

Unternimm besser keine selbständigen Versuche weiterzukommen. Du quälst Motor und Triebwerk, es nützt doch nichts —

Flußlauf

rainy weather. The damage that occurred; one engine fire, a breakage of a cooling fan shaft as well as some sheared-off screws on a countershaft were insignificant and could be fixed by the maintenance sections within short time. Damage to the suspension did not arise, despite travelling distances of 30 to 50km. Mechanical damage such as torn off running wheels and rubber tyres, sheared countershaft screws, overridden tracks, engine fires due to fuel pipes torn off by shelling could be quickly repaired due to the favourable spare parts situation.

During the transfer of two companies of the *Abteilung* in the Dünaburg area, 85 per cent of the Tigers were ready for action. No.1 Company was in action south of Idriza. The following battle damage was reported: two broken torsion bars, failure of a steering gear and sheared countershaft screws.

Mechanical breakdowns during the first days of combat south of Dünaburg could be fully dealt with due to the spare parts and the repair situation. However, travelling 80 to 100km each day and in extreme heat was tactically demanded, and the maintenance services proved to be unable to repair the large number of broken down tanks despite working day and night. The suspension is not designed for such travel. The rubber tires on the inner running wheels loosen fairly quickly under heavy load, resulting in an increased burden for the remaining running wheels. In consequence these also wear out quickly, especially during the heat during daytime. Running with, or without, damaged rubber tyres quickly led to the destruction of running wheels, bearings and radius arms. As a result of these heavy strikes the radius arms fitted with shock absorbers break even more frequently. Such damage to a PzKpfw VI requires a maintenance time of 30 to 36 hours, even when all required spare parts are at hand. The breakage of a shock

Pages 210/211
A Tiger Ausf B, possibly from 2.PzAbt 501, being repaired by members of the crew and workshop company engineers. Both sides of the suspension have been damaged and the drive sprocket has been removed for access to the final drive. To allow easy access to the engine bay, the crew has erected a 2-ton auxiliary crane on the turret and removed the heavy engine cover plate. (Topfoto)

Below
The crane on the Faun L 900 heavy recovery vehicle was fitted with a massive counter weight to balance the load when the lifting the turret of a Tiger. At left is a 4½-ton truck fitted with a Bilstein 3-ton rotary crane (SdKfz 100) also from the workshop section. (Kadari)

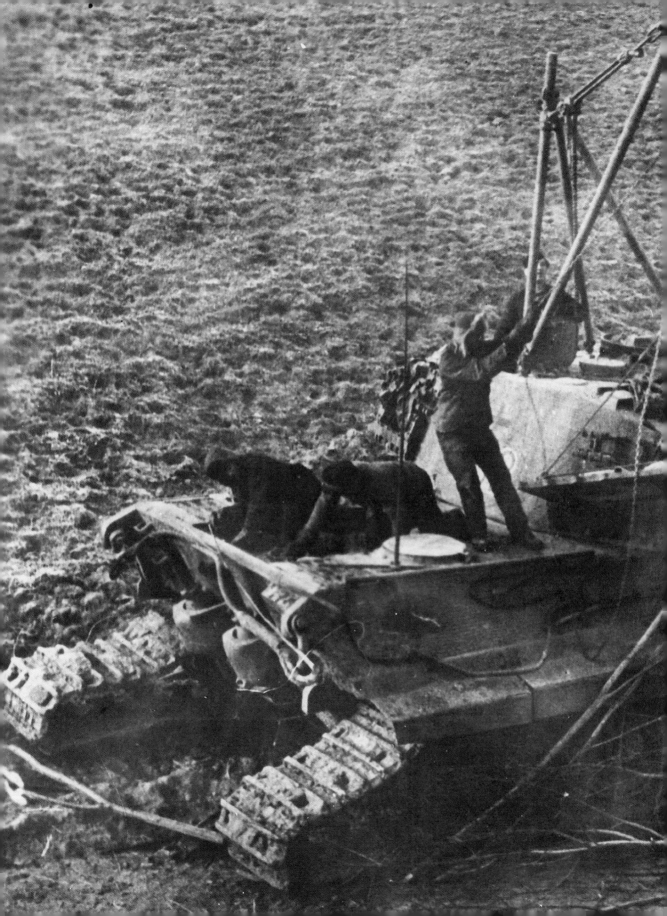

absorber assisted rear radius arm will result in the engine having to be removed. A large number of spare suspension parts are in short supply, and could not be delivered to the *Abteilung*.

The engine of the PzKpfw VI runs at a relatively high temperature and has therefore a very limited life span. Long deployments in temperatures around 35°C are technically not maintainable. Despite changing the coolers to increase flow, cooling was not sufficient at such heavy loads. Around 75 per cent of the Tigers being driven broke down due to engine problems basically caused by oil loss and carburetor fires...

...The long running also stressed the Olvar-transmission due to high temperature which led to the oil thinning to intolerant degree. This caused slow gear changes, and partly to the failure of single shift cylinders. Frequent slow gear changes did lead to a breakdown of the entire transmission. During the operations around Dünaburg most damage, due to enemy fire, occurred mainly to the final drives, drive sprockets and running wheels.

The mentioned long-distance movements led to an unprecedented consumption of spare parts. With the spare parts storage at hand the maintenance

A Tiger Ausf E from sPzAbt 505 (note the tactical number stencilled on the gun barrel) has skidded into a gulley after the driver attempted to climb an embankment. Note that the basket is missing from the rear of the turret. (Hoppe)

platoons could work eight days without any problems. Despite long-sighted planning for spare parts storage and supply the *Abteilung* could not repair their PzKpfw VI in the short term. The fact that the *Panzerersatzteillager* (tank spare parts warehouse) at Riga was moved to Königsberg and Wenden area complicated the situation. Furthermore all single railway movements within *Heeresgruppennord* (Army Group North) were blocked. Two wagons containing urgently needed Tiger spare parts from Riga to Kreuzburg was on a train for 14 days.

To overcome these transportation problems the most urgently need parts were collected by truck columns organized by the *Abteilung*.

Provision of railway SSyms wagons for the transport of Tigers was ensured by the transport officer of 16. Army.

The transfer of the *Abteilung* in the course of the withdrawal from Dünaburg to an area without a railroad connection provided new problems for the *Abteilung*. Transport of severely damaged PzKpfw VI to rear positions was not possible. At the beginning of the withdrawal three PzKpfw VI were badly damage (engine, transmission gear and suspension) making a short term maintenance impossible. All three tanks had to be towed. A further three Tigers were repaired before the withdrawal to such an extent that they could follow the *Abteilung* under their own power. The first withdrawal of the main line of resistance required to move the workshop 45km. During a two day stay it was possible to repair all broken down Tigers at new maintenance

A Tiger Ausf E from sPzAbt 506 photographed at Vinnitsa in early 1944, on the Eastern Front, undergoing a complete overhaul. It was common practice during winter conditions to remove the front outer road wheels as they could become clogged with frozen mud, resulting in a bent torsion bar. Note the perfectly applied white winter camouflage. (Anderson)

The turret of Tiger Ausf E (204) from sPzAbt 503 is lifted by a Fries 15-ton gantry crane during heavy maintenance by a workshop company. Note the turntable floor of the fighting compartment attached to the turret. The tank has received a coating of Zimmerit anti-magnetic paste. (Anderson)

sites working day and night shifts. The next withdrawal again required the workshop to be moved a further 55km. Since all the Tigers were in constant combat, the number of tanks now in need of being towed rose to nine. During the next three days stay it was possible to repair three of the most badly damaged Tigers. During the next withdrawal over 45km only six PzKpfw VI required to be towed. Some of the tanks were hauled over a distance of more than 100km. The already damaged running gear suffered even worse damage. With the exception of a few torsion bars in the centre of the hull, all the others had to be replaced.

At the beginning of the withdrawal from Dünaburg the *Abteilung* had eight SdKfz 9 prime movers fit for service. One of these broke down due to engine failure, and had to be towed since the delivery of spare parts was not possible due to the central spare parts warehouse being moved from Mitau to Königsberg. Other damage occurred including sheared-off towing eyes, distortion to vehicle hulls, broken radius arms, torsion bars and track

links were repaired by the workshop. The remaining seven tractors covered distances over 750km on towing missions. The great stress on the vehicles suspension, require four of the tractors to be completely overhauled, but this is not possible due to missing spare parts.

Recovery of broken down Tigers by a combat ready Tiger was conducted only in a few cases, when SdKfz 9 tractors were not available in sufficient numbers and the tactical situation made immediate action necessary. Towing a disabled Tiger by another Tiger is inappropriate, since most towing Tigers suffered damage to the transmission and steering gear as a consequence of the action. For recovery of broken down Tigers the *Abteilung* urgently requires the delivery of two *Bergepanther* (recovery tanks).

... The spare parts situation is still critical... The *Abteilung* is forced to use parts from the more heavily damaged tanks, or to manufacture parts if the necessary raw material is at hand or can be located.

The technical skills of the workers of the workshop platoons, the maintenance section and the maintenance troops proved to be extremely good. The expertise of non-skilled workers in the platoon was sufficient...

The level of skill shown by older drivers was good due to their long service with the *Abteilung*. A greater part of the drivers have obtained very

A mechanic attempting to get the turret down onto the mounting ring. The recuperator of this gun seems to be defective. This is a later production Tiger and has the monocular telescopic gunsight. (Panzerfoto)

Opposite
Mechanics using a Bilstein 3-ton rotary crane prepare to remove the engine access plate on a Tiger Ausf B during running trials by Henschel. The tank is painted in the late war Licht-und-Schatten Tarnung (light and shadow), a standardized three-tone colour system painted with small dark yellow dots which were intended to simulate the effect of light sparkling through foliage. The paint scheme was applied to production tanks at the Henschel plant. (Gruber)

good knowledge and experience in maintaining and repairing the PzKpfw VI Tiger. This is possibly due to the fact that all drivers assist in all repair works. Doing so, they learn a lot about the tank and mechanical operation and the cause of failures. In the period of calm, between mid-April and mid-June 1944, the drivers, mechanical personnel and technical officers received instruction on different areas such as engine, gearbox, and steering mechanism.

The new drivers sent by Germany are theoretically well-trained, but not experienced enough to drive the PzKpfw VI. Any additional practical training in the field is not possible due to the limited supply of fuel and spare parts.

The gantry cranes proved to be effective when the frontline was stable, and the workshops could remain in the same location. In times of mobile warfare this equipment was a burden to the *Abteilung*, since tractors have to be kept ready for road transport and special railway wagons for rail transport…

…Consumption of spare parts in the period 22 June to 10 August 1943

Consumption	Spare parts carried for 40 Tigers
Seven engines HL 230	Four HL 230 engines
Nine engines HL 210	--
Eleven transmissions, complete	Four complete transmissions
…	
47 drive sprockets	Eight, drive sprockets
26 idler wheels	Four, idler wheels
93 double running wheels	Four, double running wheels
220 single running wheels	80 single running wheels
…	
290 rubber tyres	80 rubber tyres…

This most interesting field report unveils the many problems found during the deployment of the Tiger tank. A complex weapons system like the Tiger required a great deal of maintenance. The basic establishment with spare parts was exceeded fourfold by the consumption. Many units reported a continual lack of spare parts and as a remedy, many damaged Tiger were cannibalized.

Recovery

German tank units had recovery vehicles as an integral part of the workshop company (*Panzerwerkastattkompanie*), according to KStN1187b. This company had three SdKfz 9 tractors and one SdKfz 9/1 *schwere Drehkrankraftwagen* (heavy tractor with rotating crane). This organizational structure was originally designed for a regiment equipped with PzKpfw III and IV and was barely sufficient.

The new Tiger units were issued with the same workshop company structure. This equipment proved to be no more efficient for the recovery of broken down heavy tanks, neither by number of tractors nor by their towing

capacity. Specialized armored recovery vehicles were available, forcing the units to improvise.

A Tiger, damaged and immobilized in the combat zone, had to be recovered at any price. The obvious solution was to tow a Tiger with another Tiger, but this was officially forbidden. The delicate gearbox system and steering mechanism of the towing Tiger could easily be damaged, leading to a further loss. As with many orders, it was frequently ignored.

The sophisticated and very heavy Tiger required special measures in repairing. Heavy-lifting equipment included a portable 15-ton gantry crane, a 10-ton crane mounted on a Faun heavy truck for lifting the turret and a SdKfz 9/2 mounting a 3-ton Bilstein traversable crane for engine removal. The sheer weight of the required spare parts needed adequate transport capacity.

Recovery of broken-down Tigers:

Normally towing a disabled Tiger on a firm road or terrain can take place using two SdKfz 9 heavy tractors. In addition, the heavy tractor is powerful enough to tow a Tiger using rigid tow bars. Longer towing distances cannot be carried out by using one tractor, since the weight of a Tiger will push it off the road. For this reason another tractor has to be connected to the tank with tow ropes to assist the first SdKfz 9. Thus the rigid tow bar tractor will be kept under control.

When towing a Tiger over mountain passes with steep inclines and twisting curves the Tiger has to be restrained by a heavy vehicle (or better a PzKpfw III), otherwise the Tiger will run off the road during descent despite the two SdKfz 9 tractors...

It was also possible to recover a bogged-down Tiger from soft terrain using one PzKpfw III... The recovery of a Tiger by a PzKpfw III from the combat zone over distances of 1 to 3km was also possible. So far an attempt to recover a Tiger with another Tiger has not been successful, since adequate rigid towing equipment is not available. The towing bracket fitted to the rear of the Tiger is unfit for this job...

The recovery of a broken-down Tiger was only possible with great effort. Towing a Tiger using one SdKfz 9 or one PzKpfw III was not always possible as revealed by the loss of five Tigers in very deep mud on one day.

Two or three Famo tractors coupled together were used to recover the disabled tank while under fire. Under these conditions any rule was ignored to achieve the recovery of the valuable Tiger.

In the field, units were inventive and wherever possible captured enemy tanks were pressed into service... a very effective measure. However, from 1943 all German units were instructed to deliver all captured tanks to higher levels. Here the valuable KV-1 or T-34 tanks were used to outfit *Beutepanzer* (recovery companies) at army level.

Left and below
It was standard practice to use three sZgKw 18t (SdKfz 9) heavy half-track tractors to tow a Tiger Ausf E. Recovery teams, often working under fire, salvaged a great number of broken down tanks which would be returned to maintenance units and be repaired ready for action. (Anderson)

A Tiger Ausf E (224) from sPzAbt 505 being prepared for rail shipment. Steel cables have been shackled to the towing eyes on the front of the tank to allow SdKfz 9 tractors to pull the vehicle on to an SSyms railway wagon. Note the simple rain cover fitted over the cupola. A rack to carry additional track pins had been fitted to the front plate. (Anderson)

By November 1943, a new organizational unit was authorized, the *Panzerbergekompanie* (tank recovery company), according to KStN 1189. This specialized unit was held in reserve by the army. The first two platoons were intended for assisting units equipped with light tanks (Pzkpfw III and IV, and StuG III) and were issued with nine SdKfz 9 each. The third platoon was intended for supporting Panther and Tiger units. Theoretically, this platoon was to have been equipped with nine SdKfz 20 *Bergeschlepper* 35t (recovery tractor) and three 65-ton flatbed trailers. Indeed, this was the *Bergeschlepper* that was never produced. Since this was common knowledge, the KStN offered a solution in a footnote trailer that stated:

All recovery units planned to be equipped with *Bergeschlepper* 35t (SdKfz 20), or with T-34 or KV-1 are to be equipped with sZgkw 18t (SdKfz 9) instead, two SdKfz 9 will replace one *Bergeschlepper* 35t (SdKfz 20)

In an after action report, sPzAbt 503 reported experiences with the *Bergezug* (recovery platoon) dated 10 October 1943:

8) *Bergezug:*
The *Bergezug* is of utmost importance to a *Tiger-Abteilung*. To assist the worn-out SdKfz 9 tractors, the *Abteilung* converted a damaged Tiger E to a *Bergetiger*.

The tank has a long crack in the lower hull but is still in running condition, the turret is inoperative. The *Bergetiger* has been used in action with good results.

The heavy tractors show a lot of wear. All too often up to four tractors had to be coupled together, this repeatedly led to the rear and frontal cross beams shearing off the chassis, where the tow couplings are fitted. To reinforce the rear cross beam the workshop welded bracing made from 25mm thick metal from a railway wagon. Further diagonal beams were welded into the frame. The frontal cross beams were reinforced by U-beams...

...Since new tractors are apparently not available, the *Abteilung* urgently sent requests for more spare parts...

When the Heeresgruppensüden (Army Group South) invaded the Crimea, the famous Asov heavy engineering facility near Rostov was pressed into German service. The large halls, equipped with heavy lifting gear allowed work to be carried out all year round. (Anderson)

The Bergepanther (SdKfz 179) was a purpose-built tank recovery vehicle. A large box-shaped superstructure, which housed a 40-ton capacity winch, was mounted on the chassis. Deliveries of the SdKfz 179 began in January 1944, and every operational Tiger unit would eventually be equipped with two of these vital recovery vehicles. (Netrebenko)

Supplying a Bergepanzer

The introduction of the new PzKpfw V Panther, forced the *Heereswaffenamt* to improve the situation of the recovery sections. The proposed SdKfz 20 (*Bergeschlepper* 35t) did not enter production. As a temporary move, four Henschel VK36.01 prototypes (allegedly fitted with a winch) were issued to the new sPzAbt. Guderian ordered the development of a recovery vehicle based on the PzKpfw V Panther and a certain percentage of the current production run were to be built as *Bergepanzers*. The vehicle should be powerful enough to tow a medium tank and was fitted with a jib-boom crane to facilitate the changing of an engine and transmission. A 40-ton winch was installed, together with a large hinged spade blade at the rear to assist with the recovery of a bogged-down tank.

The first vehicles were delivered without the winch and rear spade.

As the first Tiger unit, sPzAbt 501 received two *Bergepanther* by January 1944 and by February *Abteilungen* 506 and 509 were similarly equipped. By August 1944, all sPzAbt were equipped with two *Bergepanther*.

The *Nachrichtenblatt der Panzertruppen* 12/44 published a short experience report of a medium tank *Panzerabteilung*:

...Due to terrain unfavourable for tanks the companies were split in small

combat groups of two or three tanks. This resulted in very severe problems for the workshop companies and the small number of available recovery vehicles. After the loss of an sZgkw 18t (SdKfz 9) due to mechanical failure and a sZgkw 12t (SdKfz 8) hit by artillery, a Sherman was captured in running condition during the fighting south of Florence. This Sherman was modified by the workshop and has been in use since end of August. The Sherman was in action continuously... Since usage of this vehicle as a *Bergepanzer*, losses of disabled tanks blown up by own forces were significantly reduced... By June, these losses amounted to 61 per cent, by July this was reduced to 31 per cent... These numbers clearly prove that all Panzer and *Sturmgeschützabteilungen* must be issued with *Bergepanzer*. Tank recovery vehicles can keep many precious tanks from being lost.

The *General der Panzertruppen* in his response:

The shortage of recovery means and often spare parts is a fact the troop has to face. In case a sufficient allotment of *Bergepanzer* is not possible, the troop has to help itself, as it happened in this particular case. The troop has to recover bogged-down or damaged tank at any price, the needless destruction must be avoided... it has emerged in this report from an army group that the troop has no feeling for the responsibility they have for the tanks commissioned to them.

The large spade mounted at the rear of the Bergepanther would be lowered into the ground to act as a brake when the crew was using the winch to a recover a vehicle. The pulling power of the winch could be further enhanced by using a system of pulleys. A massive wooden beam and a 2-ton jib-boom crane completed the recovery equipment. (Netrebenko)

Some examples:

1. Five Panthers under the leadership of a lieutenant cross a heavy duty bridge at high speed too close together. Two Panthers break through and because of the lack of recovery vehicles they have to be blown up.

The lieutenant should have directed each tank to travel in single file over the bridge and at low speed.

2. One tank becomes stuck in a swampy meadow. After the battle a second

The Bergepanther was the most powerful tank recovery vehicle (TRV) in service during World War II. Here a captured vehicle is being used at a British military vehicle trials establishment. However, towing a 65-ton Sturmtiger using one Bergepanther would have been a difficult task. (Panzerfoto)

tank approaches without testing the ground. This tank also becomes stuck. Both tanks have to be blown up.

The commander of the second tank should have tested the ground before starting the recovery…

This report clearly shows the importance of armoured tank recovery vehicles, and certainly the ruggedness and quality of the US-built Sherman tank.

Under Fire 8

The entry of such a powerful tank on the battlefield came as a shock to Allied troops and at the same time as a challenge for the skilled soldiers and the engineers in the German Army. The ordinary Soviet soldier feared two vehicles: the *Sturmgeschütz* – and the Tiger tank – and there are numerous reports describing whole Russian tank units retreating after recognizing these types. Soviet military authorities published pamphlets with hints on how to damage or destroy the tank. After Operation *Citadel* the OKH published a letter detailing such a Soviet pamphlet:

The damageable parts of the German 'T-VI' and methods for its destruction

I. Running gear
The front and rear idler wheel, the running wheels and the tracks are the most important parts for the tanks mobility… Fire with AT or HE rounds at the wheels or tracks – and the tank will stop… Mount three or four mines on a plank, fix a rope to the plank, camouflage it and yourself and wait for the tank to come. When it passes you, pull the plank under the track…

II. The upper or lower side armor
…Near the rear idler wheel the fuel tanks are located. Between those the engine is situated. Fire with 76, 57 and 45mm AT gun at the lower side armour plate with either AT or HE round. The tank will catch fire and will blow up…

IV. Direct vision slots
On the turret two loopholes for firing small arms, two vision slits and five more on the cupola can be found… the driver's visor is situated in the front plate. Fire with all weapons at the slits and the optics…

A late production PzKpfw Ausf E identified by the single headlight fitted to the front of the superstructure. The crew has camouflaged the tank very carefully. By late 1944, patrolling "Tank Buster" attack aircraft were a constant danger. A hit has ricocheted off the front armour plate leaving an indentation and destroying a large area of the Zimmerit coating. (Münch)

The commander of a Tiger from sPzAbt 505 appears to be directing a group of infantrymen. The earlier drum-type cupola had a number of disadvantages, the worst being a vertically opening hatch. (Kadari)

V: The turret and the cupola

The cupola is one of the most easily damaged parts. Fire at it with AT and HE rounds with guns of any calibre, and the cupola will be put out of action. Throw hand grenades and incendiary bottles inside the damaged cupola...

VI: The gun and the MGs

In the turret the gun and a coaxial MG are mounted. In the front plate, there is a ball-mount MG. The weapons are used for aiming the main gun. Fire with all...

VIII: Slit between turret and hull

Between the hull and the turret bottom is a 10mm slit. Fire with all...

It is clear that close combat against advancing tanks is most dangerous. Many of those hints depended on determined and fearless soldiers. The Soviet Army had many.

The 198th Infantry Division captured a Soviet lieutenant of an anti-tank rifle company on 22 January 1944. The following excerpts are from his interrogation:

On 19 January 1944, a Soviet Army lieutenant from Rifle Regiment 86 was found injured in a farmhouse…

Company strength and armament:
The AT rifle co. has 24 men and 12 AT rifles (type "*Digtjarjov*"). Each rifle has 40 rounds… The company commander is authorized to select the best and strongest soldiers out of the battalion… During an attack, the AT riflemen advance with the leading elements.

Information about the AT rifle and ammunition:
The 14.5 mm AT rifle "*Digtjarjov*" (PTR-D) weighs 16kg and is 196cm long. A new type of 14.5mm AT rifle with a five round magazine was recently issued and is named after the inventor "Ssimonov" (PTR-S), weighs 20.3kg and is 210cm long. The standard AT round will penetrate steel plate 3.5cm thick at a range of 50m. The prisoner knows of a new type of ammunition with much better penetration…

The most feared tanks are the "Tiger", "Panther" also the "Ferdinand" assault gun…

Recovery missions had to be accomplished at all costs, even at night. An SdKfz 9 is reversed up to the rear of a Tiger to allow engineers to fit rigid towing bars. Another two tractors will be attached to haul the tank back to the workshop for repair. (Münch)

Pages 230/231
Tigers from sPzAbt 505 are prepared for an assault. A group of 10 or more infantrymen are gathered behind the turret for transport. Both tanks have minor damage to the track guards. (Anderson)

Two Tigers from sPzAbt 505 on the Eastern Front, the vehicle at left is an early production Ausf E with smoke grenade dischargers fitted on the turret. The tank, to the rear, is fitted with the later type cupola. (Kadari)

Right

A Tiger Ausf B from sPzAbt 503. German tanks were fitted with an escape hatch for each crew member, which helped to keep losses in personnel down to a minimum. (NARA)

In April 1943, the Soviet supreme commander of the artillery (at that time Marshall Voronov) published an instruction for defeating the Tiger tank. German official bodies captured a copy and published it in an article in the *Nachrichtenblatt der Panzertruppen* Volume 4:

> Gun commanders and gunners have to carefully study the weak points of the enemy tanks. They must know, what projectile at what range will be correct to destroy the tank... The heavy tanks of the mentioned type can be defeated by HE shells only when hitting the running gear, the turret ring or the gun.

Type of gun	Firing HE shell	Firing AP shell
45mm gun M 1937	Running gear, turret ring, gun	Side plates, turret ring, rear at 200m range
45mm gun M 1942	Running gear, turret ring, gun	Side plates and turret ring at 500m, front at 100m range
57mm gun	Running gear, turret ring, gun, rear at 600m range	Front at 500m range

The T-34/85 was a logical development of the proven Soviet-built T-34 medium tank. A larger turret mounting a more powerful 85mm gun was fitted on a basically unchanged hull and chassis. The T-34/85 was referred to in German publications as the T-43. (Panzerfoto)

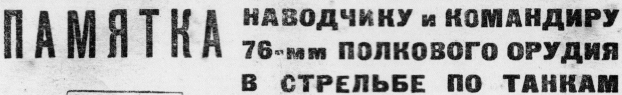

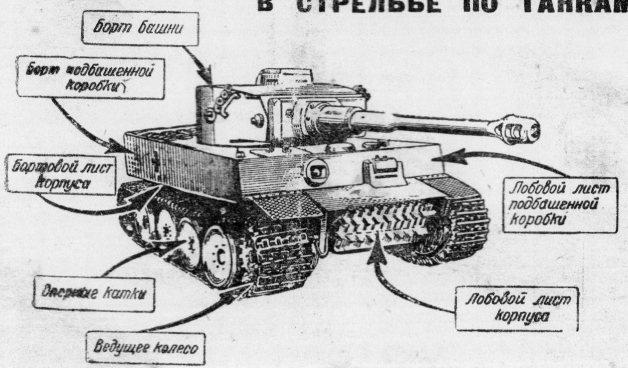

ГЛАВНОЕ УПРАВЛЕНИЕ КОМАНДУЮЩЕГО АРТИЛЛЕРИЕЙ КРАСНОЙ АРМИИ

ПАМЯТКА НАВОДЧИКУ и КОМАНДИРУ 76-мм ПОЛКОВОГО ОРУДИЯ В СТРЕЛЬБЕ ПО ТАНКАМ

Борт башни

Борт подбашенной коробки

Бортовой лист корпуса

Опорные катки

Ведущее колесо

Лобовой лист подбашенной коробки

Лобовой лист корпуса

The Soviet Army published this leaflet to instruct anti-tank (AT) teams and tank gunners as to where to attack the weak points of a Tiger tank. (Anderson)

Gun	Weak points	
76mm gun M 1942	Running gear, turret ring, gun	Side plates, turret ring and rear plate at 700m, front at 100m range
76mm AA gun	Running gear, turret ring, rear at 500m range	Front at 700m range
85mm AA gun	Running gear, turret ring, rear at 100m range	
122mm field gun M 1931	Front, sides at 1,000m, Turret ring and rear at 1,500m range	
152mm howitzer M 1937	Front, sides at 500m, Turret ring and rear at 1,000m range	

Before opening fire, gun commanders and gunners have to wait until the enemy tank reaches the favourable range.

In 1944, the Soviets started production of a new heavy tank. The pre-war KV-1 was developed as a "breakthrough" tank, and its appearance on the Eastern Front came as a shock to the German invaders.

While the T-34 influenced German tank development by the revolutionary design of the type, the KV-1 had a similar performance but was larger and had better armour protection.

In the January 1945 issue of *Nachrichtblatt der Panzertruppen* Volume 4, a translation of a new Russian pamphlet was published:

…Translation of a Russian pamphlet for commanders and gunners of 7.62cm guns regarding firing at tanks

Armour-piercing sub-calibre tracer shot

1. The armour-piercing sub-calibre tracer shot must only be used against heavy tanks and *Sturmgeschütze*. It is strictly forbidden to use it against light or medium tanks, if ordinary armour-piercing shots are at hand.

The unknown Russian artist possibly had access to the Tiger of sPzAbt 502, which was captured by the Soviet Army in late 1942. The position of the German cross and the PzKpfw III-style turret basket was unique to this tank. (Anderson)

По возможности открывай огонь по танку, когда он под-ставит бок (займёт к тебе положение под углом от 30 до 90°)

УЯЗВИМЫЕ МЕСТА НЕМЕЦКОГО ТАНКА

Пушка

Корма башна и корпуса танка

Борты

Основание башни

Ходовая часть танка

Ходовая часть танка, основание башни и пушка ЯВЛЯЮТСЯ НАИБОЛЕЕ УЯЗВИМЫМИ МЕСТАМИ

Тяжёлый танк Т-6 („Тигр")

1. Бронепрожигающим снарядом:
— только по бортовому листу корпуса — 500 м.

2. Осколочным снарядом:
— по ходовой части — 1000 м.

A drawing showing where to fire on a Tiger tank with 7.62cm high-explosive (HE) and armour-piercing (AP) rounds. HE rounds should be fired at ranges up to 500m at the gap between running gear and hull. AP rounds up to ranges of 1,000m directly at mechanicals such as the drive sprocket, idler wheel or the tracks and the running wheels. (Anderson)

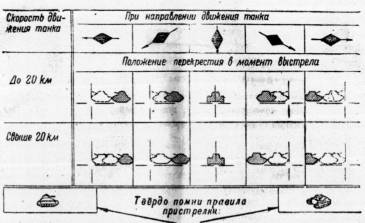

НАВОДИ В ТАНК ТАК:

1. Если первый выстрел [при таком] движении танка дал боковое отклонение позади цели больше чем на одну фигуру, вводи поправку в угломер на измеренное отклонение, но не менее чем на 0-05, командой: «Левее (правее) 0-00, огонь».

2. As a last resort the sub-calibre shots must be always at hand for the fight against heavy tanks.
3. Direct engagement is effective only at ranges up to 500m. At ranges further than 500m usage is banned.

Standard armour-piercing shot
1. Use the armour-piercing tracer shot and hollow charge shot against light and medium tanks. Shoot at all weak points.
2. When using it against heavy tanks, fire at sides, rear and running gear

Standard HE shot
With this shot fire only at the running gear, turret ring and gun barrel. Use impact fuse…

This pamphlet shows that the Soviets also had to restrict usage of their hard-core ammunition. It is interesting that armour-piercing sub-calibre tracer shots (which, according to German records was not a sub-calibre round but a hard-core AP shot) were to be used only at ranges up to 500m. Comparative German shots were far more powerful.

Probably the most advanced heavy tank of its time, the IS-3 known as the "Pike". The powerful 122mm gun, thick armour (up to 120mm) and low silhouette, made it a battle winner (Panzerfoto).

Conclusion 9

Much of what has already been written about the Tiger has emerged from the evaluation of technical reports and on the personal diaries of ex-servicemen. However, there can be some inaccuracies with memoirs written after the war, even when this was done rather shortly after the conclusion of hostilities. Alas, the passing of time can sometimes influence the accuracy of historical fact.

The reputation of the PzKpfw VI Tiger Ausf E or B ostensibly lives on battlefield successes and the perceived "invulnerability" of the vehicle. The Tiger is frequently described as being "too heavy, too unreliable".
However, many of these facts are seldom backed by historical data.

It has been my intention to approach this subject by using archive material only. On the one hand this was easy, much of the respective material can be found in the archives of *Bundesarchiv* (Germany), NARA (USA), and The Tank Museum, Bovington in the UK. On the other hand, I found out that many important areas of Tiger operation were not covered satisfactorily. While there are many reports dealing with the Tiger E in combat during the years 1943 and 1944, little detail has survived of operations in the final months of the war. Documents of similar quality relating to the PzKpfw VI Ausf B Tiger II are scarce and here I have had to rely on the personal memories of ex-crew members.

In September 1942, the first combat action with the Tiger Ausf E, which took place south of the Lake Ladoga, was a total fiasco. Being aware of the difficult, swampy terrain the few Tiger in service with sPzAbt 502 at that time were sent into action and impeded by the heavy ground. One Tiger was destroyed in the battle and the others all heavily damaged.

As detailed in Chapter 6, the battlefield qualities of the Ausf E would soon be demonstrated – especially on the *Ost* (East) Front. The success of the heavy

Members of a Bergezug (recovery crew) are carried on a Bergepanzer VI in service with sPzJgAbt 653. The only armament fitted on the vehicle was a Maschinengewehr 34 (MG 34) machine gun, carried in a ball mounting on the front plate of the superstructure. (Münch)

By late 1943, the Ferdinand (SdKfz 184) mounted the most powerful tank gun in service. The 8.8cm PaK 43/2 powerful enough to destroy any known enemy armour long ranges. The vehicle was not fitted with a close-defense weapon such as an MG. This could be a problem, if the vehicle and crew was isolated from their own infantry. (Anderson)

tank battalions was impressive. The sPzAbt 503 reported the results of 78 days combat in and around the Kursk salient on 10 October 1943:

Successes:	
	501 Enemy tanks
	388 AT guns
	79 Artillery-guns
	7 Enemy aircraft

Losses:		
	Officers	2
	Clerks	1
	NCOs	12
	Other Ranks	29

	Total	44

Own tank losses:
7 Destroyed
6 to 12.2 and 5.7cm guns
1 to Molotov-Cocktails from a Soviet close-combat team
1 by fire from own *Sturmgeschütze*
3 from direct hits by artillery
1 due to the right-hand final drive becoming jammed (Tank destroyed by crew)
1 due to engine failure (Tank destroyed by crew)
1 by a shell penetrating the hull (Tank destroyed by crew)
4 by shells penetrating the hull between the suspension and track cover causing large cracks (returned to the Reich for complete overhaul).

During the period of the report the *Abteilung* were supposed to have an average of 12 Tigers operational each day. Due to technical breakdowns during the march from the workshop to the combat echelon we had an actual daily average of only 10 Tigers...

It is hard believe, that the unit could destroy such a large number of enemy tanks with possibly ten, perhaps twelve tanks being combat ready each day.

The report does not quote the enemy's loss of personnel. Many German units were to count or estimate only the number of fallen enemy soldiers for their records. The total number of Soviet soldiers killed in action during World War II was horrendous.

However, in the West the Tiger tank could not be deployed to such an advantage. There was of course a decisive difference between launching a Tiger assault over the vast open plains of central Russia (ideal tank country), or the Appenine Mountains in Italy. Furthermore, the now better trained and equipped Allied tank forces were able to deal with this menace despite the lack of a truly heavy tank.

Also, the numerical superiority of enemy forces in both the West and East was of importance. In a report by the US military, an officer of a sPzAbt is quoted after his capture as seeing a huge "junk yard" of destroyed US Sherman tanks:

...a Tiger can easily shoot up 10 American panzers. You, however, always had an eleventh US panzer waiting to attack...

The following bulletin of the armoured forces was released in February 1945:

...Conduct of battle by enemy tank forces in the West:
1. American and British forces always try to avoid the open and mobile tank v. tank combat, because they feel inferior in regard to flexible leadership and the

In September 1943, three Bergepanzer IV were issued to sPzJgAbt 653 after the end of Operation *Citadel*. By December 1943, the vehicles had been rebuilt in Austria as Bergepanzer Elefant and two were delivered to the unit when it returned to the Eastern Front. The vehicle shown is thought to be the one which served with 1.Kp/sPzJgAbt 653 in Italy during 1944. (Münch)

effective range of our tank guns.

2. Tank assaults will be launched by the enemy only if these can be backed by sufficient own artillery and air force fire. By observing the early fire from our AT guns and tanks, enemy forces try to destroy these by combined fire of their artillery... and their tanks held back for fire support.

3. When attacking, American forces frequently use smoke, he covers the open flanks of his own tank assaults by smoke and lays screens only recognized by his own tanks, AT guns...

4. The enemy tanks will be deployed only in close cooperation with infantry. Even small attacks with tank groups of five to eight tanks will be accompanied by infantry.

5. In the course of the German winter offensive enemy counterattacks to even a very small extent were launched against our routes of advance. These weak, but numerous attacks... are aimed to find places or a section where no German tank is deployed.

6. Smaller scale advances with tanks will be launched during the night as well...

This appears to be a copy of a German tactical directive issued during the *Blitzkrieg*.

The high number of German victories was, possibly, the result of the high degree of tactical skill used by commanders in the field. In the *Wehrmacht* it was standard practice to train a soldier to a rank two levels higher than that actually required. In this way, losses among the officers and senior NCOs could be substituted.

German mission-type tactics were proven especially on the Eastern Front. Assaults against massed Soviet troop formations holding fixed positions could often turn into a surprising success, against an enemy which was truly revered by German forces as being "tough" and "courageous and bordering on suicidal".

Towards end of the war the supply situation worsened day-by-day. A radio message from AOK 2 to *Heeresgruppe* Weichsel dated 11 March 1945 reveals:

Panzer and *Sturmgeschütz* – situation most tense due to continuous desperate defensive battles.

...7.PzDiv has 12 Panzer (six combat-ready), 28 StuG and 18 *Jagdpanther* V (combat-ready)

...4.PzDiv has 36 Panzer (eleven combat-ready), six StuG and four *Jagdpanther* V (combat-ready)

...4.SS-Pol-PzGrenDiv has two Panzer (1 combat-ready), 42 *Jagdpanzer* IV and 12 StuG (combat-ready)

...SS-PzAbt 503 has eight Panzer VI (Three combat-ready)...

...Further course of the fighting depends decisively on the supply of Panzer and StuG, especially Panzer V, *Jagdpanther* V and Tiger. At the time the army has only 35 Panzer V and eight Tiger, of which 14 Panzer V and three Tiger are combat-ready for fighting enemy heavy tanks...

Many heavy tanks had to be blown up by their crews. All too often a tank broke down due to light damage or lack of fuel, but could not be recovered because there was no specialist equipment. Major Schmidt of sPzAbt 507 reported such a case on 11 May 1944.

…PzAbt 507 reports following correction to the message on 1 April 1944:

The PzKpfw VI lost was not chassis No.250838, but chassis No.250831, which broke down on 29 March 1944, south of Jecierna. Reason for break down: Tank became stuck in a swamp, recovery was not possible and was blown up by the crew…

By early 1945, if the Tiger was responsibly deployed in action with full knowledge of its capabilities and shortcomings, units could achieve incredible results, even in hopeless situations. But if Tiger units were dispersed or sent to action as a platoon or sometimes alone, the attack was likely to be a failure.

The range of missions for the Tiger was limited by other factors. The complex vehicle required comprehensive maintenance and care even after many years of experience with the type in frontline service. Many components including the final-drive units were very to prone to damage being unable to withstand long periods of running. If these components were not maintained correctly, or if spare parts were not available, the number of breakdowns increased.

The Jagdtiger (SdKfz 186) armed with a 12.8cm PaK 80 L/55 gun was the heaviest armoured vehicle to enter service in World War II. The vehicle has been abandoned by the crew in a deserted German town in the last days of the war. The Jagdtiger appears to be undamaged having possibly suffered a mechanical breakdown or simply run out of fuel. (US Signal Corps)

sPzAbt 502 reported on 1 September 1944:

…Panzer VI

Issued	45
Combat-ready	19
In short term repair	8
In long term repair	18
Troop morale:	Confidential
Special problems:	Acquisition of spare parts is difficult due to the combat situation. For this reason combat readiness for 50 per cent of the combat echelon is in doubt.
Degree of mobility:	80 per cent
Combat value:	Fully prepared for every attack or defensive mission…

Similar situation reports read the same.

As a result the legend remains untouched. The heavily armoured, powerfully armed and mobile Tiger tank will remain a fascinating subject, for the crew who felt safe, an excellent subject for the Nazi propaganda machine, and truly awesome to many enemy tank crews.

Porsche proposed a simplified running gear, to save materials, for both PzKpfw VI Ausf B Tiger II and Jagdtiger. No Tiger II was ever produced with this suspension but 10 Jagdtiger were completed. The vehicle shown here is fitted with narrow transportation tracks and is at the Haustenbeck test facility. Note the early production Tiger Ausf B in the background. (Panzerfoto)

Variants

Although not the main subject of this book, reference to variants based on the Tiger (H) and Tiger (P) must be included.

Adolf Hitler, and the German ordnance office were keen advocates of improved versions based on the existing tank designs. Over the course of World War II the most ubiquitous terms in this context were *schwere*, for heavy and *Sturmgeschütz*, for assault gun. Hitler was always fascinated with "heavier", "more powerful" and "indestructible" versions, demanding them even before the respective main battle tank which was to provide the basic chassis was ready for combat. However, the word *Sturmgeschütz* influenced the mindset of the leadership. The rôle for this important type of vehicle was often confused with that of the *Panzerjäger* (tank hunter/destroyer). By 1943, the terms *Sturmgeschütz* and *Panzerjäger* had become interchangeable. All this resulted in the wish for a somewhat archaic "Battering Ram" type of weapon, a vehicle strong enough to withstand fire from any enemy weapon and pave the way for advancing German forces.

Ferdinand

The first major development on the chassis of the heavy Tiger tank was the Ferdinand. Actually, this design originated from a failed tank programme.

Bogged-down in soft ground, a Jagdtiger is inspected by US troops. The vehicle was difficult to operate in combat and any mistake by the commander or driver could lead to it being abandoned. Recovery of the 72-ton Jagdtiger would be virtually impossible, even by the powerful Bergepanther. (US Signal Corps)

Two sZgKw 18t (SdKfz 9) haul away a broken down Tiger Ausf E from an unknown sPzAbt in Italy. German recovery sections were very efficient and a countless number of damaged tanks were recovered in very difficult conditions, even under enemy fire. (Münch)

When the production of the Porsche *Typ* 101, or Pzkpfw VI Tiger, VK 45.01 (P) was halted due to insurmountable technical problems, the authorities had to admit that Krupp had already fulfilled their order to manufacture 100 hulls for the heavy tank.

By September 1942, a new concept for a *Sturmgeschütz mit 8.8cm (Lang)* was introduced. Hitler and his advisors had decided that existing VK 45.01 hulls should be used for the production of a turretless vehicle fitted with extraordinarily heavy armour (200mm at the front) and the powerful 8.8cm PaK 43 (L/71) gun.

Apparently the mechanical problems with petrol-electric drive were finally solved. In appreciation of Dr. Ferdinand Porsche, his first name was chosen as the official designation. Production had started by the end of the year and four days before the proposed delivery date the final vehicle was completed at the Nibelungenwerke, Austria.

The Ferdinand was issued to sPzJgAbt 653 and 654, which were subordinated to sPzJgRgt 656. The regiment also incorporated a *Sturmpanzerabteilung* and two *Panzerfunklenkabteilung*(PzFklKp) issued with remote-control demolition vehicles.

On the battlefield, a total of 502 enemy tanks, 20 anti-tank guns and 100 other artillery pieces were destroyed by Ferdinand equipped units. Only 39 were lost to enemy action.

Two have survived; one is preserved at the US Ordnance Museum, Fort Lee, Virginia, USA. The other is on display at Kubinka Tank Museum, Moscow, Russia.

Bergepanzer VI

The excessive weight of the Ferdinand required a well-equipped recovery section. For this reason three recovery tanks were built on PzKpfw VI Tiger (P) chassis and all were issued to sPzJgAbt 653.

Sturmmörser

This was the result of plans to build a mobile 38cm rocket launcher with sufficient armour protection and utilized the chassis of the Tiger Ausf E. Originally designated as *Sturmmörserwagen 606/4 mit 38cm RW61* (also known as the *Sturmtiger*) a total of 18 were built by mid-1944 and deployed on all war fronts. Two of these impressive vehicles are preserved, one at Deutsches Panzermuseum, Münster, Germany and the other at Kubinka.

Jagdtiger

By 1943, the idea arose to supply the troop with a *schwere Sturmgeschütz* heavy assault gun. This was to be fitted with a 12.8cm gun and maximum armoured protection. The chassis of the Tiger B was chosen, but this had

The Sturmmörser (also known as the Sturmtiger) was mounted with a 38cm rocket launcher designed to destroy complete buildings or concrete fortifications. The idea of such an assault tank was born from experience gained during the heavy fighting in urban areas around Stalingrad. The tactical value of the type during the defensive battles for the Reich at the end of the war is questionable. A total of 10 Sturmmörser were built on the chassis of the Tiger Ausf E. (Anderson)

to be lengthened by 30cm to house the massive gun. The weight of the finished vehicle exceeded 70 tons. Quite naturally, the 12.8cm gun ensured the destruction of any enemy armour at ranges of up to 3,000m. The massive armour (20cm thick on the front of the superstructure) gave an extraordinary level of protection for the crew. Mobility of the vehicle can only be described as very limited. The commander of a unit issued with *Jagdtiger* remembered that he was hardly able to lead the unit since he was always busy with finding suitable roads for his tanks.

Three *Jagdtiger* have survived the war; one is in The Tank Museum, Bovington, UK, another at Kubinka and one is preserved at the US Ordnance Museum.

Surviving Tigers

The aura surrounding the Tiger tank was so strong that quite a number have survived.

PzKpfw VI Ausf E Tiger

Kubinka Tank Museum, Moscow, Russia
Military-Historical Museum, Lenino-Sengiri, Russia
US Ordnance Museum, Fort Lee, Virginia, USA
Musee des Blindes, Saumur, France
Vimoutiers, Normandy, France (in public)
The Tank Museum, Bovington, UK

PzKpfw VI Ausf B Tiger II

December 44 Museum, La Gleize, Belgium
The Defence Academy of the British Armed Forces,
     Shrivenham, UK (on loan to Bovington)
The Tank Museum, Bovington, UK
Thun Tank Museum, Switzerland
Patton Museum of Cavalry & Armor, Fort Knox, Kentucky, USA
Deutsches Panzermuseum, Münster, Germany

A Tiger Ausf B being prepared for battle in the autumn of 1944. The type was the most powerful tank to enter service in World War II. The Tiger Ausf B required careful and constant maintenance, also a skilled driver was essential. Vehicle reliability has been described as adequate. (Münch)

INDEX

A company of PzKpfw VI
Ausf B Tiger II heavy tanks
from sPzAbt 503 are lined
up in preparation for a
propaganda film.

In February 1944, all SdKfz 184 Elefant (Elephant) self-propelled guns were deployed to Italy. The vehicles proved to be unsuitable for the rural conditions of the Italian battlefield. Many were lost but all the surviving Elefants had been returned to Germany by January 1945.

A US Army recovery team examines a disabled Tiger Ausf B. The right-hand track has been damaged by a well-aimed shot, immobilizing the heavy tank. As a repair or recovery was not possible the crew abandoned the tank even though it was ordered to destroy it so that the vehicle would not be captured intact by the enemy. (US Signal Corps)

Acknowledgements

I would like to express my appreciation to the following individuals who have provided help, advice or photographs.

My special thanks go to Karlheinz Münch, who allowed me access to his wonderful collection of photographs. Further material was provided by Henry Hoppe. My eternal thanks go to the late Tom Jentz, the undisputed expert on the history of German armoured vehicles.

I also recommend the outstanding *Panzer Tracts* which provides in-depth knowledge of German armour. Further titles by this author include *Germany's Tiger Tank, Combat Tactics*, and *Panzertruppen*: Volumes 1 & 2.

Other important books on this subject have been written by Karlheinz Münch (the history of German *Panzerjäger* and *Sturmgeschütz* units) and Wolfgang Schneider (the history of German heavy Panzer units).

Thomas Anderson, November 2012.